Internal
Affairs

ALSO BY KATHLEEN NEVILLE

Corporate Attractions: An Inside Account of Sexual Harassment with the New Rules for Men and Women on the Job

Internal Affairs

THE ABUSE OF POWER, SEXUAL HARASSMENT, AND HYPOCRISY IN THE WORKPLACE

KATHLEEN NEVILLE

McGraw-Hill

NEW YORK   SAN FRANCISCO   WASHINGTON, D.C.   AUCKLAND   BOGOTÁ
CARACAS   LISBON   LONDON   MADRID   MEXICO CITY   MILAN
MONTREAL   NEW DELHI   SAN JUAN   SINGAPORE
SYDNEY   TOKYO   TORONTO

McGraw-Hill

A Division of The **McGraw-Hill** Companies

Copyright © 2000 by The McGraw-Hill Companies, Inc. All rights
reserved. Printed in the United States of America. Except as permitted
under the United States Copyright Act of 1976, no part of this publication
may be reproduced or distributed in any form or by any means,
or stored in a data base or retrieval system, without the prior written
permission of the publisher.

1 2 3 4 5 6 7 8 9 0   DOC/DOC   9 0 9 8 7 6 5 4 3 2 1 0 9

ISBN 0-07-134256-7

*The sponsoring editor for this book was Mary Glenn, the editing supervisor
was John M. Morriss, and the production supervisor was Elizabeth J. Strange.
It was set in Minion by North Market Street Graphics,
317 North Market Street, Lancaster, PA 17603*

Printed and bound by R. R. Donnelley & Sons Company.

McGraw-Hill books are available at special quantity discounts to use
as premiums and sales promotions, or for use in corporate training
programs. For more information, please write to the Director of Special
Sales, McGraw-Hill, 11 West 19th Street, New York, NY 10011. Or contact
your local bookstore.

This publication is designed to provide accurate and authoritative information in regard to the subject matter covered. It is sold with the understanding that neither the author nor the publisher is engaged in rendering
legal, accounting, or other professional service. If legal advice or other
expert assistance is required, the services of a competent professional
person should be sought.
—From a Declaration of Principles jointly adopted by a Committee of the
American Bar Association and a Committee of Publishers.

 This book is printed on recycled, acid-free paper
containing a minimum of 50% recycled, de-inked fiber.

FOR JEFF

Contents

Gender References

Please note that in an effort to simplify the presentation of material in this book there may be certain situations where the offender may be referred to as a male or "he" and the offended party as a female or "she." Sexual harassment can be, and is, experienced by either sex and can also occur with the same sex.

Acknowledgments

This is only my second book, but I already know that "it takes a village" (a very understanding and patient one!) to bring a book to life. Because this was a particularly difficult book to write due to its subject matter and the controversy surrounding sex in the workplace, I needed much help from the beginning to the end of my journey through the *internal affairs* of today's workplace. I thank all those employees, and the companies they work for, for letting me share their stories with you in this book.

I thank McGraw-Hill, particularly editor Mary Glenn and editorial director Susan Barry, for believing in the importance of providing information on this widely debated topic. It has always taken courage and foresight in the publishing business when it comes to the issue of sexual harassment and sexual misconduct in the workplace. They both have shown it, and I appreciate their personal commitment. Thank you to John Morriss, who makes the process of "putting a book together" a true pleasure. And more thanks to others at McGraw-Hill including Claudia Riemer Boutote and Karen Auerbach. I am also deeply indebted to Judy Duguid for all her help and assistance in editing this book. I also thank my agents Helen Rees and Joan Mazmanian of The Helen Rees Agency for understanding what my work in this field means to me.

My own commitment to this book began years ago when I first started working inside companies. In fact, every single time I spoke with a company or an employee about sexual behavior in the workplace, I was reminded how important it is that we exchange information. For years now, we have been in desperate need of information that we can all use. *Internal Affairs* came about because I felt that people needed to know about what others were experiencing, thinking, and doing about this issue. There seemed to be many widely scattered parts of this so very complicated issue of sexual harassment and sexual misconduct in the workplace, and somehow we needed to piece them together. Despite the high profile of this issue, finding helpful and useful direction on managing such problems remains an intimidating and often overwhelming task for most of the working world. Let's face it, this issue is not taught in business school or college or even high school for that matter. We are struggling with this behavior in our workplaces, so it is without question that we will need much more information for the twenty-first-century workplace of tomorrow. It seemed that a book that didn't focus on just legal angles or pure academic perspectives, but found instead a central point of view that considers everyone—both companies and their employees—rather than one side *or* the other, was needed. I thank everyone for the numerous parts and pieces they provided me so that I could put them together in this book to get some sort of "bigger picture" of this issue.

I thank those people who have given this issue a great deal of thought and have expressed those thoughts publicly (like Imus in the Morning, for example!). I have included in this book many contributions from a number of sources—from consultants, professors, lawyers, business leaders, human resources specialists, and, most important, working people. I have also included comments from some very thoughtful articles, columns, and writings that offer tremendous insight into this issue, an issue that is at the forefront of today's workplace and world.

I would like to thank Mitsubishi Motors Manufacturing of America and Mitsubishi Motors Sales of America for allowing me, a few years ago, an inside perspective of their companies. There are many fine people working for both companies, and I believe we all had a chance to learn a great deal from the ordeal. I hope that many other companies around the world will benefit from your experiences. I would also like to thank the Reboul MacMurrary, Hewitt, Maynard & Kristol law firm of New York for making the journey a good one.

A very special thank-you to Dr. Sandor Blum, Boston, and to Dr. Marion Gindes of New York for their genuine interest, valuable time, and extensive knowledge in addressing workplace behavior. Thanks also to Dr. Elissa Perry at Columbia University for her help and assistance in the area of organizational behavior and theory. I especially thank Burke Marshall of Yale University Law School for his dedication to civil rights and support of others involved.

I would like to thank my dear friends Susan Doscher and Hiroshi Wald for their expertise, friendship, and support in researching this project. Thanks also to Meg Masuno at Stanford University and Candice Atherton for research assistance.

I would also like to thank the law firm of Coudert Brothers, especially Richard Reilly for his invaluable insight, legal guidance, friendship, and endless help over the past five years.

And thank you, Frank Mankiewicz, Melanie Luftig, Jana Kravitz, Daniella Cracknell, Barbara Suess, Thea and Henry Killeen, Karel Amaranth, Lynn Sochon, Louise Baudoin, Amy Lipton, Gail Blanke, Robin Abramson, Mary Civiello, Linda Wolf, and, always, Donna Ent, for your constant support in all that needs to be done, and your belief that each of us can make a difference.

I thank my special family, including all four of my brothers, Rich, Bill, Tim, and Jim, for all their help and support in providing not only their important male perspective but their input too. And thank you to my nephew, JJ, for figuring out, at only seven, that the theme of this book seems to be about "people needing to be fair." I couldn't have said it any better myself.

I especially thank my lifelong editor, my mother, Millie Neville, for her help in editing and proofreading. Thank you for always making sure that the Wilson background is in everything I do. And speaking of Wilson, thank you, Kay Ness, for always believing in the importance of sharing information through books. And, Dad, you are with me in every effort. Thank you.

I also would like to remember two very special people who greatly impacted my life and those who knew them—Larry Attisano and Linnea Brady Massey. Your goodness will always live on.

And from the bottom of my heart, thank you to the joy of my life, Dr. Jeff Latham.

Sexual Harassment and Sexual Misconduct in the Workplace

How Did We Get Here and Why?

Sexual harassment (sex′ u al ha rass′ ment), *n.* 1. something sexual that happens at work that shouldn't happen unless you clearly want it to happen, and even if you want it to happen, but nonetheless, it still shouldn't happen if someone else at work doesn't want it happening in front of them. What constitutes "sexual" is subject to change. 2. unwanted sexual advances esp. by an employer or superior that might cause a chain of events that can destroy a company's reputation, create chaos inside an organization, ruin people's health, well-being and careers, and cost as much as 50 million dollars.

KN

Coming to Terms with Sexual Harassment

If you have something of importance to say, for
God's sake start at the end.

—Sarah Jeannette Duncan

WHAT A MESS, INDEED!

While I was headed home one night, a stranger seated next to me on the rush hour train out of Manhattan abruptly dropped his newspaper down to his lap, shook his head, and muttered to me, "What a mess!"

I looked up from what I refer to as my latest "train book." (My definition of a train book is usually a piece of fiction, as in the James Patterson, David Baldacci variety, and one that *never* has anything to do with my line of work.) Since the stranger had spoken to me, at the very least, I thought, I needed to look at the "mess" he was referring to and let him know if I agreed. I glanced down at the article he had been reading. It was a front-page story about a brokerage firm accused of having something called "a Boom-Boom Room" on its premises. According to the article, some employees were alleging that the room—whose name sounded as if it had been thought up by clever Neanderthals—was being used for the specific purposes of sexual antics. Women at the 125-year-old "white shoe" brokerage firm had come forward with the allegations. I already knew the story. I had spoken to someone at the brokerage house a few days before. Definitely, if true, it was a real mess.

"Yes, it is," I replied as I nodded gravely. The stranger wanted to talk. I was impressed about how much he seemed to know about the problems relating to the issue of sexual harassment in the workplace. He spoke knowledgeably about the challenges of educating people and specifically mentioned what he was concerned about at his own company. What made our conversation more unusual than it already was is that commuters in and out of New York City often don't converse during their trek home from work, let alone open up about sexual misconduct in the workplace.

As he talked, I listened quietly. This was ironic. I had spent the entire day with several mid-level and senior executives in the conference room of their Wall Street firm discussing this very same topic. The discussion on the train was far more revealing than the one on Wall Street.

The stranger went on to mention that his company had a "program," but that the company did training only once a year. (I was happy to hear that the company did it at all.) Certainly they didn't have anything as outrageous as a Boom-Boom Room, he said, but he felt there were a few guys he worked with who still weren't getting the message. They took, what he termed, sexual risks at work. That seemed to bother him.

As he prepared to get off at the next stop, I thought I should come clean and tell him I truly understood what he had been saying—that I worked with individual companies to address sexual harassment in their workplaces. "Actually *all of this*," I pointed to the now crumpled-up Boom-Boom article sticking out of his briefcase, "this is what I do." Not exactly a great description of my life's work, but I've always had a difficult time conveying, in just a few words, what my work is all about. After all, sexual harassment—and all that is required to identify, resolve, and prevent it—are complicated issues. Over the years I have witnessed some shocking "internal affairs" inside all kinds of companies—sexual scandals that would raise the eyebrows of even the most steadfast skeptics. I've had up-close views of internal affairs that have rocked the core of businesses to the point of no return. I have seen the impact of sexual misconduct be so damaging to organizations, reputations, and individuals that even a nonbeliever in the necessity of sexual harassment policies would be forced to think twice. And, of course, I've seen the money that's been spent. I have watched companies write out huge checks to conceal what they will sometimes admit are their own "dirty little secrets," or what I have termed for the purpose of this book *internal affairs*.

"Oh," the stranger said slowly and then added, more lightly, "I'll bet you could tell me a story or two." Oh, I could. Definitely. It was his corporate voice talking next. "Look, to me, it's business," he said as he pointed to himself for a second. "I don't want to work with people, or worse, have people who work for *me* be stupid enough to pull this kind of thing. Who wants that? And besides," he added with a shrug as he gathered up his coat and draped it over one arm, "it's just wrong." I wondered if he might have thrown in the last remark having just learned that I have a personal stake in eliminating those "wrongs." Perhaps not.

As he stepped out into the aisle to wait for the train to slow to a stop, he asked me how it was that I got into such an "interesting" line of business. Without even noticing that I didn't answer, he went on. "Well, talk about good timing," he said as he started down the aisle. "You are certainly in the right business at the right time. Nice talking to you," he called over his shoulder as he made his way out.

GOOD TIMING AND A FEW GOOD STORIES

My stop was next. All I could think of as I walked from the train to my car was the conversation I had just had. Like others who are committed to educating men and women in the workplace, I have spent more than fifteen years of my life trying to get the working world to take a good hard look at the issue of sexual harassment from a business perspective. Sexual harassment costs companies millions and millions of dollars, and yet the business sector has always balked at tallying up the total. For me, getting companies to acknowledge both the immediate and the far-reaching financial consequences of sexual harassment is one of my goals; getting them to realize the terrible price men and women pay personally for experiencing it is another.

As I drove home, I thought back to my earliest days in this business, and how, most times, it seemed all but impossible to truly convince legislators, judges, opinion leaders, and employers that sexual misconduct in the workplace was prevalent. Getting someone inside the Beltway, or in the court system, or in the business sector, to recognize and then consider, what irresponsible human behavior was doing to the core of the business world seemed like a long shot. This is certainly not true anymore. Building awareness of sexual harassment is no longer a problem—the media have taken care of that. With each front-page story or prime-time exposé detailing charges of sexual harassment, more people have come to the conclusion that there is a problem, perhaps even an epidemic. *Now, the impact of sexual misconduct inside corporations and the solutions available to eliminate it must get our immediate attention.*

THEN AND NOW: THE CHANGE OF FOCUS

As far back as twenty years ago, sexual harassment was mistakenly regarded as a woman's issue. Along with that assumption, sexual harassment was supposed to be a rare and random occurrence. It was one of those "victim things," doubters claimed, usually happening to unsophisticated women, those professionally unqualified and socially unprepared for interacting with men on the job. I know better.

The man on the train was a messenger of the times. A human marker for where we are. Thanks to his unsolicited testimony, he was solid proof that the working world was doing more than merely reading about sexual harassment. Old thinking seems to be history.

Today, survey data show that up to 60 percent of corporate America is making some sort of attempt to address sexual harassment in the workplace, often in the form of policies and sometimes even training. On the surface, these efforts seem to say more about corporate liability than personal accountability. And to some degree that may be true. There is a striking difference between a corporation's mandatory educational efforts and an individual's decision to be accountable for his or her own sexual behavior at work. To use a marketing term, the *target audience*—the person on the street (as in the working man or woman)—has to be involved in the problem-solving aspect of the transformation in order to achieve any degree of positive change in attitude or culture.

Remember the 60's phrase: "If you're not part of the solution, you're part of the problem"?

THE FOCUS ON CHANGE

Harassment stories in the news, lawsuits ending with record-breaking settlements and awards, even history-making sex (or is it sex-making history?) scandals in the White House don't mean all that much without workers thinking about their own roles and their own behavior on the job. Company by company, from one worker to the next, the relevance of the issue must hit home. The only way to truly manage this blight on the workplace is for all of us to recognize the extent to which it exists and to learn better ways to minimize its presence and impact.

Which brings me to the point of this book. From top management down, companies need to take a "helicopter ride" over corporate America, looking closely not only at the damages "down there" on their own turf, but at what is occurring at other companies, both large and small. Once we all have a good grasp of the extent of the problem, we need to start trying to make some changes, both as individuals and as organizations. The man who has always called his assistant "Sweetheart" may start thinking the time is right to call her by her name, instead. The woman who has made it a practice to shop for sexual partners in her workplace perhaps will think about the ways her personal pursuits at her company aren't really personal or private. Even CEOs—or, say, even the leader of the free world—might think twice about their own personal accountability when it comes to the issue of sexual harassment.

This book deals with the issue of sexual harassment from a number of different vantage points. Chapter 1 gives you an overview of what people are thinking regarding sexual harassment in the workplace. The differences of opinion clearly show why this issue is so controversial and why the definition of *harassment* is so unclear for most of us. Chapter 2 addresses the legal aspects of sexual harassment, and Chapters 3 and 4 discuss the "who and why"—*who* are the people at fault for harassing in the workplace and misusing their power, and discuss some possible reasons *why* they are doing it. These chapters also look at those people who raise false claims and why they pursue that course.

Chapter 5 offers almost a tear-out definition of sexual harassment and how it shows up in the workplace. Chapter 6 walks you through an actual case, an anatomy of a lawsuit, and shows how all the issues of sexual harassment are deeply woven together. Chapter 7 goes inside companies in which top-level CEOs have been accused of sexual harassment and shows the web of consequences that results when senior executives put personal desires before corporate responsibilities. You will be able to get a better perspective on how companies view and respond to charges that can and do affect an entire organization.

Chapter 8 reports on the real financial cost of sexual harassment, and examines some of the corporate programs that are misfiring in so many corporations. It also describes why companies use a quick-fix solution to the problem of sexual harassment and why such solutions don't get to the root cause of the problems. Chapter 9 recognizes the challenges foreign companies and their American workers face when both companies and employees work on U.S. soil under U.S. civil laws.

Chapter 10 has advice for employees and employers when they are faced with a complaint of sexual harassment. This chapter points out why there is no such thing as a harmless complaint. Chapters 11 and 12 discuss what the stakes are for everyone when it comes to sexual harassment in the workplace and offers advice for those who would like to do a better job of being both personally and professionally responsible for contributing to a better workplace.

An Appendix has been included that offers a few brief case studies, various sources of guidance, summaries of the most significant sexual harassment cases, the text of Title VII of the Civil Rights Act of 1964, and a sample sexual harassment policy.

So I share with you now "a few good stories," a.k.a. case studies, and hope this information will motivate, even encourage, you to make whatever changes necessary in your own working life, within your own organization. By realizing the significant impact each of us has within our own workplace, we can also realize the tremendous opportunity we all have to help create positive and healthy environments. Individuals make up organizations, and those same individuals contribute to what ultimately becomes the distinct culture of an organization. Even if just one person is engaging in inappropriate sexual behavior, his or her actions instantly become part of the company's environment and corporate reputation. Just ask the brokerage firm that made the front page.

I want to take you backstage for a tour behind the scenes, into corporate America's internal affairs. We will examine a series of cases, much like virtual "Boom-Boom Rooms," which will include inside perspectives on some of corporate America's hidden daytime dramas. In fact, in the following chapters, you will meet several of the more notable stars.

KATHLEEN NEVILLE

August 1999

CHAPTER 1

Sexual Harassment Today

The startling state of affairs

"I did not have sexual relations with that woman, at least, not the kind, I think, that you think I had."

—Tom, Dick, Harry, or Bill

REDEFINING THE UNDEFINABLE CRIME OF THE CENTURY

MAIN STREET

I was recently called into a small, but rapidly growing, organization where a woman claimed that a new executive, Jerry, was pressuring her to sleep with him. Each time that he tried to coax her into having dinner with him, or to go with him in his car, or to have an after-hours meeting with him in his office, it was, he claimed, his way of acting as her mentor. He wanted to help her have a chance at getting one of several business positions that would soon become available. He told her that she had no idea how to politically position herself with management. It was a growing company and she had a great deal to offer. But without his help, no one else would know that. He had an "in." She didn't. Once he had a clear idea of the position she wanted, he could talk to the head of operations and give her a good recommendation. With every invitation to discuss her taking advantage of the doors that *only* he could open for her, Jerry pitched her for sex. He was unhappily married, he told her, going through some rough times, but he wanted her to know that he had never cheated on his wife before.

She didn't have sex with him. Instead, she reported him. The higher-up that she reported it to was now meeting with me. The company had asked him to give me an overview of the harassment claim. Before we talked about the claim itself, he thought that I should have a better profile of the woman who had complained. "She looks like a Barbie doll," he told me, irritably. "She wears too much make-up and dresses too provocatively," he said. "I told her she should tone it down. Then Jerry wouldn't be so interested in her, you know, sexually." The manager was agitated. He didn't have time for

1 5

this. He kept shaking his head. She's a big problem. Yes, he thought that Jerry probably did exactly what she said he did. But it was a crucial time at the company. Frankly, he needed Jerry for the reorganization. And what he also needed now was a plan to take care of this sexual harassment claim. One, he said, that would send her on her "merry way."

WALL STREET

I was just finishing up an internal investigation of sexual harassment inside a Wall Street firm. I was about to interview the last witness, the man being accused of sexual harassment, Carl. As soon as he was told the reason I was there to see him, the color started to drain from Carl's face. There had been many serious charges against this senior employee, and they came from a number of female employees. The claims had been thoroughly substantiated by numerous witnesses, both male and female. Even the CEO had witnessed this employee's sexual misconduct. The head of the company also told me this employee was singularly responsible for making more money for the firm than anyone else in his entire division.

The alleged harasser was well-groomed and articulate. "I can't believe this is happening to me," he blurted out. He volunteered to tell me all about himself. He was a family man with two children and was involved with his son's soccer team. Of course, then, reports of his bad behavior—rampant requests for sex, his morning narrative in front of his staff about his distaste of "faggots," his racial slurs about the African-American women in another department resenting him because he was a successful white guy, his descriptive movie reviews of the pornography he watched, and the vulgar comment that Maura, the receptionist, had "nice tits"—must not be true.

Carl continued, "I love my wife and I would never be involved with someone else, at work or anywhere." In fact, the more he thought about it, he was morally outraged at *other* men he worked with at the firm.

Other guys at the firm were always organizing outings that included strippers and, well, he might as well tell me, even "prostitute types." They went to clubs. I wouldn't want to hear what went on *there.* Two other coworkers even had sex out on the lawn in front of the exclusive resort where the last company function was held. Without any prompting whatsoever, my new friend Carl ratted on everyone he worked with at his firm.

But I couldn't get Carl to open up regarding the specific charges that were leveled against him. Instead, he talked about other matters. "I believe in God," he said in a lowered voice. "I am actually very religious. It has always been an important part of my life." It was good to be able to talk about this with someone, he said. As he talked, I thought hard about what he was saying so that I had a clear picture of the kind of person he wanted me to believe he was. I asked him about the report of his trying to slip his hand through the armhole of one of the female vice president's sleeveless blouses after she had taken her suit jacket off during a warm July meeting. He flinched, but just for a second. Never happened. He acted surprised that a couple of people actually said they saw it happen *and* said that they heard him say that he just wanted "to get a feel for what was up there." He wondered what those people could possibly have against him.

I continued my questioning. Did he have a practice of asking Sarah, a twenty-two-year-old direct report of his, if she had sex the night before with her boyfriend? Did Carl tell her he "was mad because *he* wasn't getting any at home"? Outrageous, he said. It's totally twisted around. That's not what happened. He had asked Sarah to meet him at the office one Saturday to help out on a project. They couldn't get everything done during the week. Sarah concocted this story because she was angry about having to work on a Saturday. It's an industry practice, working on weekends. Support staff know they need to be committed to their jobs, but they never are, said a frustrated Carl. Sarah is young, doesn't understand this business. Not cut out for it. Carl shook his head. It's so hard to find *good people.*

OK—WHAT'S GOING ON?

From Main Street to Wall Street, these are challenging times for a working nation. The sexual behavior of the 131 million working people in the United States has never been examined more closely or sparked more heated controversy than now. During the past few years, sexual behavior has become an important workplace issue. Becoming sexually involved with someone in the workplace, willfully, willingly or not, has emerged as one of the most conflicted and complicated issues of the decade, encompassing issues of social, sexual, personal, professional, economic, and even political importance.

Evidenced by the fact that even the President of the United States can be sued for sexual harassment, sexual behavior at work stands as one of today's top workplace perplexities. The 1990s has seen a virtual explosion in high-profile sexual harassment cases, from Clarence Thomas to Bill Clinton. Yet while the politicians make front-page news, it is corporate America that has had to deal with the day-to-day realities of sexuality in the workplace. More importantly, corporations have been left the task of turning lessons learned into practical game plans for managing both sexual surges and ensuing power plays of everyday working people. What we have is a workplace that is stuffed to overflow with ambiguous rules of conduct, diverse corporate cultures, opposing personal beliefs, sharply differing attitudes, and a general blanket of uncertainty regarding this business of sexual behavior. While research polls, surveys, and studies show that sexual misconduct in the workplace is growing, much of corporate America remains in denial. Many still question why we are trying to run human sexuality out of the workplace—that sexuality in the workplace does little harm. As far as the courts are concerned, there is just as much discussion regarding whether current civil rights laws can, or even should, protect workers from sexual discrimination as well.

In fact, lawyer Richard Dooling, in a 1998 article for *The National Law Journal,* said that he thought that the "he-said-she-said" disputes of sexual harassment litigation are about to become even more intractable. "Soon, employers will be absolutely liable for all misconduct, moral failings, personality disorders, sociopathologies, medical infirmities and 'disabilities' of every employee in their hire."

The European view of the state of U.S. companies and sexual harassment reflects the notion that litigation is out of control. In the July 1998 article of *The Economist* entitled "Men, Women, Work and Law," Americans were sharply criticized for overregulating the workplace. The publication contends that although Americans say they want the government off their backs, they also rush to legal remedies for social problems that most countries leave to individuals to sort out. Referring to significant Supreme Court decisions made in 1998, it points out that "in a series of decisions . . . [the Supreme Court] greatly extended the scope of anti-discrimination laws in a way that will not only increase the burden on employers but could well turn the American workplace into the most highly regulated in the world."

A prominent attorney, who specializes in defending companies against claims of harassment, went beyond just criticizing the laws. He went straight for the throat of those at the center of this issue. If you were to ask him what he thinks is going on with the issue of sexual harassment today, he would say that nothing is going on. At least, nothing that is *real*. It's all "noise" cranked up to a loud pitch by a chorus of greedy, disgruntled employees looking for a way to stick it to their companies. He purports that the statistics provided by the Equal Employment Opportunity Commission (EEOC) and by various studies and surveys are exaggerated, most of the claims are false, and the majority of the plaintiffs are, well, crazy. Some claims might be valid, but they are few and far between. He further believes that both false and questionable claims, regardless of their merit, are supported by special-interest groups with agendas of their own.

He stated all this before the beginning of a presentation I was attending in the fall of 1998. I had assumed it would be a rather high-brow legal overview of the issues I deal with inside companies. Because almost all of the complaints I am involved with are resolved before actual courtroom litigation, I wanted to hear some other perspectives from those who handle complaints that have found their way to court. The panel on the stage of the lawyer-packed conference center consisted of an equal number of plaintiff attorneys and corporate attorneys involved in sexual harassment cases. The purpose of the program was to discuss the current "state of affairs" of harassment in the workplace from both sides of the issue.

The attorney, who had taken over the panel discussion before it had formally started, wasn't about to yield his place to the moderator until he felt that he had made his points. Before anyone else said anything, he wanted to make it very clear to anyone who would listen that the statistics that are "out there" are not facts, and shouldn't be taken as such. False claims are wrongly counted as legitimate incidents of sexual harassment these days, he said. Because the financial awards being won by these cases are greater than ever, so are the number of frivolous complaints.

His final point was that all of this "sue your employer for being insensitive" business was costing everyone, especially companies. A tremendous amount of companies' profits are spent to defend employers against such charges. Employees are being given a license to extort those they have gone to work for, and the media just keep feeding and misleading the public about who is really at fault. The "nutcases" have the ball, and companies are afraid to attempt any aggressive defense strategy to get it back. Some simply have to drop their hands to their sides and just let the plaintiffs score.

When he finished, the panel began its long and rather colorless discussion of legal strategies for these cases. No one challenged the pre-presentation "speaker." If the plaintiff attorneys had wanted to effectively counter the defense attorney's statements at any point in the program, they didn't seize the opportunity. Either they didn't have any backup facts to support their side of the issues, or they didn't want to bother. I sensed it was a little of both.

When I left the auditorium that night, I felt I had just left a time warp. What I had heard reminded me of the way claims of sexual harassment were looked upon back in the seventies and eighties. It was common then to use a legal defense strategy that was certain to punish and embarrass anyone who brought a complaint into the courts. The two-for-one special of hammering the plaintiff du jour, while sending out a clear message to all others that the personal costs of filing a claim of harassment would be too high, was a prevalent practice. I didn't like to hear, firsthand, that some continued to view this kind of harsh attack as an effective defense strategy.

Unlike the conference attorney's assessment of the state of affairs both in and out of courts, I believe that *the problem is real.* My perspective comes from time spent with real working people with real problems who have suffered real injuries. I see companies that are doing their very best to manage this issue, but are basically operating without a standardized manual. The problem is real, yet I believe that litigation is often the last—and, unfortunately, least effective—resort. Because I often serve as a bridge between employees and management, I believe in the effectiveness of the resolution process. And just as important as conflict resolution is the commitment to educational efforts once an internal crisis is past. The twin objectives of creating a fair environment and keeping open future opportunities for resolution combine to form both the present solution and the ongoing goal. At least, they do for me.

Over the years, I have been closely involved with several hundred sexual harassment disputes. Conflict, especially when it has to do with sex and power, is especially devastating and far-reaching. Almost everything that is important—job, money, reputation, family, and future—is on the line for those involved. Ask the general manager of the New York Mets baseball organization, Steve Phillips, how he felt when he was charged in 1998 with a sexual harassment suit by a dismissed female employee. Phillips had to admit to his employer, his wife and two children, and the general public that he had had "a consensual sexual relationship" with the employee who had charged him. Phillips had to turn his GM responsibilities over to someone else and take a temporary leave of absence to get his personal life in order.

With one serious public claim of harassment, a rising star often becomes a falling star that crashes onto hard, unforgiving ground. Corporations have a lot to gain by working through these problems within the workplace where they originate instead of in the media where careers can be ruined. With any other approach, there is so much talent to lose and so much productivity that can never be regained. The workplace is the most appropriate arena for problem resolution, providing the company has the proper training and internal mechanisms to address the issues. When a claim is resolved at the company level, there is every opportunity to stop the harassment, discipline the harasser, make necessary changes in reporting relationships, and protect the company and its employees from outside scrutiny. In-house resolution is ideal for today's companies, and many companies are starting to figure that out. The costs of developing in-house programs and procedures to handle claims promptly and thoroughly amount to a few cents per worker versus the high costs of court proceedings. Most employees have no interest in suing their employers. They know the results can be more devastating than the grievance. What employees want is for their employer to respond honestly, impartially, and compassionately to their claims.

When a claim cannot be settled through the internal channels a company has established, the claim can end up in full-blown litigation. Despite the media spotlight on high-profile or lurid cases, taking a claim of sexual harassment to court is not exactly an everyday occurrence. Over 94 percent of all sexual harassment cases are settled *before* decisions are rendered in court. If you are in the small percentage of those that get to court, not only will you probably be making case law history somewhere, but you will find that today's judges are much more knowledgeable on the ways of the working world. While clearly unenlightened views still exist, both sides of sexual harassment court

DISCRIMINATION

Number of discrimination charges filed with the Equal Employment Opportunity Commission in 1995: **87,500**

Breakdown of those cases:

Disability discrimination   Race bias

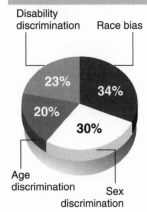

23%   34%

20%   30%

Age discrimination   Sex discrimination

Source: Equal Employment Opportunity Commission
Note: Figures add up to more than 100% because some cases involve more than one type of discrimination.

Other numbers:

■ Average cost to defend a discrimination case: **$100,000**
■ Average settlement in discrimination case: **$15,000**
■ Total amount of money awarded to Title VII plaintiffs: **$154 million**

Source: Atlanta attorney James Demetry

Chart 1
EEOC claims during the past seven years [1992–1999]. (CNN/TIME, March 14, 1998)

disputes are treated much more fairly, these days, by the court process and by the judges themselves.

Even though most cases are settled out of court, in 1996, American workers brought a whopping 23,000 lawsuits alleging workplace discrimination to federal courts, more than doubling those brought in 1992, according to the U.S. Courts' administrative office. Job discrimination lawsuits have risen by at least 20 percent a year. In fact, sexual harassment cases filed with the Equal Employment Opportunity Commission have more than doubled over the last seven years (1992–1999). (See Chart 1.) Just imagine the sexual harassment that still goes unreported.

LET'S HEAR IT FROM THE CROWD

When I conduct seminars on sexual harassment in companies all across the country, I learn just as much from the participants as they do from me. I get to find out what they are thinking. Most employers believe that there is no place for sexual harassment in the workplace. Reasonable men and reasonable women who work for these "reasonable companies" feel the same way. Remember the man on the commuter train? I believe he represents the majority of us in our thinking. But there are other opinions (that tend to be louder) out there that we all should be aware of because they reveal how much more we need to do to educate our workforce. To give you an idea of what is out there, here are just a few of the opinions I have heard while conducting internal employee seminars in companies around the country:

- Companies are just pretending to help us with a policy. If we actually complained, they wouldn't do anything about it. They are just "covering their behinds."
- There is still a class system within companies. Only the important people in the company have any rights. The rest of us are just throwaways.
- Someone is trying to ruin the sexual balance that men and women have reached in the workplace by pushing this antiharassment policy. (Usually the person who voices this opinion indicates that the "someone" is a feminist or a special-interest group.)
- As employees we want to be left alone. Don't fix something that isn't broken. If you try to change the way men and women work

together and interact with each other, you will somehow destroy the products being made.

- It's even worse for creative people who need a loose environment to do their best work if strict antisocial policies are forced upon them in their workplace.

- Sterilization of the workplace is deadly for morale *and* for business. You can't build or deliver good products and services from a purified and lifeless environment.

- Sexual conduct in the workplace is a private matter. If someone wants to date or sleep with someone he or she works with, it is his or her business. It is not the company's business or someone's staff or coworkers' business, and it should not be the concern of the company's clients or vendors. If those who engage in this kind of conduct are married and get caught, it is between them, their spouses, and God. (Including God in the "three-way workout" plan has been very big this past year, for some reason.)

- Women, if they want, should be able to use their sexuality in the workplace. It's a way to equalize the power. Men do certain things to get ahead in their work. Women have *their* ways.

- Sexual tension makes the workplace more interesting. Just like they do in coeducational learning environments, women dress better and are more motivated when men are around. (Remember, I'm just the messenger, here.)

- People who claim sexual harassment are psychotic, deranged, hysterical, unstable, nuts, crazy, delusional, and paranoid. They also hate men, hate women, hate their mothers, hate their ex-husband, or are simply just *trouble*.

- People who claim sexual harassment are incompetent at their jobs. It's a lucrative way to leave a job they either are going to get fired from, are going to lose because of reorganization, or planned on leaving anyway because they are tired, old, lazy, going to open their own business, going to get married, or are already (or hoping to be) pregnant. (Remember, I'm still only the messenger!)

- Sexual harassment claims are made by those who hate or are jealous of their bosses. Resentment of taking orders motivates them to vengeful and vindictive acts. They will do anything to ruin their bosses. You can never shake a sexual harassment charge, and mean-spirited employees who launch charges know that.

- It's the "create your own golden parachute" pension plan for a worker who otherwise wouldn't have a chance to save or accumulate a lump sum of cash. If someone is in a protected class (as in over 40, with a disability, etc.), that makes it even better.

- Sexual harassment claims are an attention-getter for someone who is looking for notoriety and a shot on a talk show. The accuser is a professional victim looking to be a part of the flavor-of-the week cause.

- The government is sticking its nose in the workplace, and it doesn't belong there. It feels like the government has contracted the company to institute the "Big Brother" plan of spying on workers. What will be next?

- Feminists are behind this movement to control the workplace. This is just one more excuse for holding press conferences and a way for Gloria Allred (you know, that woman attorney in the red suit with red nail polish) to acquire more high-profile cases. Feminists are always mad at men, and this is a perfect way to show their anger.

- Plaintiff lawyers are encouraging employees to sue. It's a new version of "ambulance chasers" waiting in the company's parking lot.

- You can thank the liberals for this one!

- Men are pigs. They always have been. You'll never change them.

- Anita Hill is a psycho. She liked Clarence Thomas, and he turned her down. This is about her revenge.

- No one wants to work anymore; everyone just wants to sue everyone else for everything.

- Women only want certain men to make passes at them at work. The rest are not rich, powerful, or good-looking enough. These women are selective. Screaming sexual harassment is a way of weeding out the undesirables.

- The fashion industry is to blame. Fashion is so sexual these days that it is all anyone can think of at work. Everyone is practically naked.

- A particular kind of woman is behind this. Most women resent these troublemakers speaking for all women.

- Where is the tough skin? Women said they wanted to work, but they complain about everything.

- I mean, rape is wrong, but this isn't the same thing. Sexual harassment is a made-up offense. I just want to talk to women I work with and get to know them as people. Now I'm afraid to even make eye contact. Give me a break.

- Women want you to make a pass at them. They do everything they can think of to get your attention.

- It's out of control, and we are all going to suffer from this.

HIGH STAKES

Despite the well publicized cases of Presidents, movie stars, senators, and CEOs who have been accused of sexual harassment, people are continuing to take risks in the workplace. They are still having sex, pursuing sexual relationships, using sex as a power tool, and manipulating others with sex at work. They think they are taking only a personal risk, and are surprised to learn that their tryst has turned into a companywide crisis.

Just when I am sure that I have seen it all, I find myself stunned, once more, at the next set of sexual escapades I must either investigate or sort out. Society is deeply divided about the issue of acting out sexual desires, using sexual power, and exerting sexual manipulation at work.

This division keeps showing up in the form of sexual harassment complaints. Ask any group of people about any publicized case of sexual misconduct and you will get very mixed reactions: "It was the woman's fault." "He has a drinking problem—he wasn't thinking clearly." "He did it. I can tell by his eyes." "She wanted it to happen." "He did it. I can tell because he looks just like my former brother-in-law." "As a woman I know how to handle the men I work with. Too bad *she* doesn't."

MY TAKE

In devoting a significant part of my life to helping employees and employers address the issue of sexual harassment in the workplace, I've picked up on a couple of very interesting things. First of all, from the CEOs of the most powerful companies in the country to the new hires fresh out of school, most people don't know what they need to know, what they *must* know, about sexual harassment. Second, almost everyone has strong feelings about this issue. When sexual harassment in the workplace is discussed, it is with the same tone of voice that people use when they talk about politics, religion, or anything else that matters deeply to them. Sexual harassment is the one business issue we take personally. Employees have a position and often find themselves willing to defend it. But the most important observation I've made since I've been involved in helping others manage sexual misconduct in the workplace is this: *Sexual harassment unleashes powerful emotions in those who witness or experience it.*

Despite the best efforts of many companies to develop corporate policies and conduct yearly educational seminars on the subject, there is strong evidence indicating that many working people don't really know what is or isn't acceptable behavior under the law. Beyond the ever-present hurdle of getting people to acknowledge the seriousness of the problem while coaxing corporate minds to remain open to solutions, we are still looking for exactness in meaning. What is *this thing,* which some news reporters call "HAR-as-ment" and others pronounce as "her-ASS-ment"? These days, we can't even seem to agree on pronunciation, let alone definition. And that's just for starters.

Getting companies and individuals to arrive at a universal definition of sexual misconduct in the workplace seems to be the challenge of the day. As the public spotlight continues to pass steadily over corporate backyards waiting to expose the latest, darkest workplace sex scandal, the bewilderment regarding the definition seems to be growing as rapidly as the brushfire of media exposure it creates. The more we hear about sexual harassment, the more confused we seem to be about what it is.

The search for the big-print, easy-to-understand definition of sexual harassment is ongoing. We are not there yet, although we really need to be. In my first book on sexual harassment, which was published almost ten years ago, I reduced the definition down to its most basic form. The three key elements of the core definition were then, and still are, sexual *and* unwanted *and* in the workplace. In order to be sexual harassment, behavior must be sexual in nature (or sexually based), be unwanted, and occur between people who, in some way, work together. This definition gives you an idea about motive, reaction, and location.

Back in 1990, before the Clarence Thomas hearings, I very much wanted to get as many people as possible signed on to acknowledging the problem. Although the academic and legal sectors were very interested in definitions, at that time the working sector was not. Most sensible people now seem to accept this kind of basic definition without issue and understand, in theory, why it just shouldn't happen at work. Usually people think about sexual harassment in its most extreme and obvious form—as in a woman being pinned up against the wall by her obnoxious and tyrannical boss. But definitions begin to change, quite dramatically, when individuals, based upon their own world and circumstances, begin to *interpret* the definition on a *personal level.*

THE CORPORATE TAKE
JOEL

Joel, a vice president at a high-tech company, thought it was easy to see that Lennie, from the mail room, was sexually harassing women in his department. He even thought about mentioning it to human resources, but he didn't want to get involved. Within the past year, he had just been transferred to the San Francisco office. The company had sent him here to rebuild the sales force, not clean up the mess the jerk from the mail room made behind him. He hoped someone, maybe one of the women, would take it to HR. No one could miss Lennie's act. While making his daily mail rounds, he would swoop around the desks of the women at the company and make juvenile "cat-call" sounds as he stared at their legs. Sometimes, Joel could hear Lennie coming out of a woman's office, saying ridiculous things, which usually ended in "Oh, baby, you sure are looking fine, and I sure like to look." Joel just cringed when he heard Lennie coming down the hall. What an idiot! He was embarrassed that someone like that was employed by the company.

But one night when Joel ended a dinner at an expensive restaurant by suggesting to Jennifer, one of the sales reps who reported to him, that he'd like her to come back to his apartment, the notion of sexual harassment never entered his mind. Asking Jennifer to consider a sexual encounter was a personal matter between two consenting adults. They were friends. Joel felt comfortable telling Jennifer about his failing marriage. After his transfer from Ohio, his wife and children had stayed behind to finish out the school year. Once the house was sold, they would probably split up, he told Jennifer. Essentially, he was single. In fact, he could see himself having a relationship with Jennifer. She was more his type than his wife. Although he missed being close enough to get to Ann Arbor to see a football game at his alma mater, he thought the move to San Francisco was a good one— for a lot of reasons.

JENNIFER

Jennifer had been a sales representative for four years and wanted to move to a management position. At first, she was very disappointed when she heard the company was bringing a man in from Ohio to manage the department. She had hoped she would be given the job. There were no women managers in any of the sales departments on the West Coast. She thought the company was very sexist in the way it treated women sales representatives, and she was tired of it. When Joel arrived at the company, he immediately recognized those with talent. He had seen what Jennifer was capable of doing. Maybe, she thought, Joel would soon be moving to the divisional manager job, and she would get his position.

Based upon the way Joel was treating her, she felt as though she was being singled out as his replacement. She was really learning from Joel. It was exciting. She was stunned when Joel started to rub his hand up and down her back at dinner. She had no idea until then that Joel was interested in her sexually. She turned him down, but gently. She didn't want him to be angry with her, so she said that she was not feeling well. He tried to kiss her goodnight as he walked her to her car.

Now, he was leaving strange messages on her voice mail. She played a few of his messages for her friends, just to see if she wasn't overreacting. Her friends told her she wasn't. Joel asked her to travel with him to St. Louis for a meeting. She believed it wasn't necessary for her to go. Her gut feeling told her he wanted to use the meeting as an excuse to get her alone. She thought about telling him that she had no interest in being involved with him, but she was pretty sure that would put a huge strain on their professional relationship. Now she wondered if she ever had a chance for promotion, or had she been misreading Joel's attention?

She thought about what she should do. She could continue being friends with Joel and hope that he would never put her in a position that would frighten her. But that didn't seem likely. She couldn't go to human resources. Linda, the HR manager, wasn't someone she could talk to about this. Linda was always sucking up to the men. Anything they told her to do she would do. Linda didn't know what they said about her behind her back, but Jennifer knew that they wouldn't listen to Linda if she went to them to resolve a complaint. The more Jennifer thought about it, the more she realized that her options were limited, and none of them were good for her. As she sat at her desk, realizing that she would probably have to leave the company if she couldn't handle this herself, Lennie from the mail room walked in. As usual, he was going on about how nice she looked; this time, the blue of her suit matched her eyes. She wished it was only Lennie's harmless comments she had to deal with these days. She could handle Lennie. It was Joel's persistent pursuit that was making her feel physically sick. She felt like she was in a corner with no way out.

LENNIE

Working in the company's mail room was just a day job for Lennie. He was hoping to go work for his cousin in San Diego next year. His cousin had a bakery business, and he said that Lennie could do well there once things got going. Meanwhile, Lennie did what he needed to do to make a living, although he really did hate the men he delivered mail to each day. He couldn't stand the way they talked on the phone and acted so important. He felt sorry for the women in the company, having to work with those stiffs. The women were great. He loved going in their offices and seeing what was going on. There were a lot of good-looking women at the company. He let them know he thought they were hot. He was sure they appreciated it because it had to be a drag working so hard.

THE RESULTS

Within this company, three different people have three different defin-itions of sexual harassment, and they all clash. (It's not unusual for American workers to disagree about what sexual harassment is. Chart 2 shows the result of a poll that proves this point.) Because this

Poll: Americans disagree on fine points of sexual harassment

March 14, 1998

Web posted at: 9:08 p.m. EST (0208 GMT)

(CNN)—Just what is sexual harassment?

Depends on who you ask.

A CNN/TIME poll shows there is a general consensus on some issues, but the margin narrows as the boundaries between overt and implied sexual behavior become murkier.

The 1,023 respondents were divided on common social interactions such as flirting and friendly touching.

About 55 percent of respondents say it's sexual harassment if a boss asks for sex but does not retaliate if the employee rejects the advances.

It is sexual harassment if a boss . . .

Asks an employee to have sex
YES 79%
NO 15%

Insists on telling sexual jokes
YES 66%
NO 28%

Puts his arm around an employee
YES 56%
NO 36%

Flirts with an employee
YES 46%
NO 45%

sampling error: +/–3% pts.

A similar number—51 percent—said it's always unacceptable for a boss and employee to have sexual relations.

Only 56 percent of the respondents say it's a case of sexual harassment when an employer puts his arm around an employee; just 46 percent regard flirting with an employee as harassment.

And, about 54 percent of the respondents say the labeling of some interactions as sexual harassment cases clearly has gone too far.

Consensus on some issues

Most Americans agree on what constitutes the most flagrant examples of sexual harassment.

Chart 2 Americans disagree about what sexual harassment is. (CNN/TIME, March 14, 1998)

Chart 2   *(Continued)*

Consensus on some issues

Most Americans agree on what constitutes the most flagrant examples of sexual harassment.

Is it sexual harassment if a boss asks for sex but does not retaliate if employee rejects advances?

YES	55%
NO	39%

Is it sexual harassment if a boss makes sexual remarks but does not retaliate if employee objects?

YES	62%
NO	32%

Would you feel uncomfortable saying no to a male boss?

(Women who work)

YES	55%
NO	39%

Would you feel uncomfortable saying no to a female boss?

(Men who work)

YES	25%
NO	72%

The poll, conducted in February, included 413 adult men and 342 adult women who work. There is no significant difference between the views of men and women on these questions.

company had no real policy and no grievance procedures in place for Jennifer to take advantage of, Jennifer ended up taking her claim of sexual harassment outside the company for resolution. The company settled with Jennifer for $225,000, giving her essentially two years' salary and outplacement until she found another job. Joel was not fired but was transferred again. He was good friends with Jim Alcott at head-quarters, who lobbied to save Joel's job for him. It wasn't an easy task, and Jim Alcott made it clear he would never help Joel again. Joel didn't see a bonus that year, and his wife left him. It wasn't the first time Joel had become interested in someone at work. It was, however, the first time someone had complained. His wife had always known his trips out of town included a cute member of his staff. This was the end of the road for her. Lennie continued to behave exactly the same way. The company, though, began to make changes. It finally decided it needed to distribute a sexual harassment policy to employees. It also sent Linda to some classes to help her and her department better understand their roles as human resources specialists and know what to do when they received a complaint of sexual harassment.

THE WORKING CLASS AND HIGHER EDUCATION

Not every American company is like General Electric, willing or able to spend almost $800 million on training and leadership development. Corporate policies and procedures, fully staffed human resources divisions, and sophisticated educational seminars on workplace issues are not available to all American workers. In fact, workplace environments are as diverse as the people who work in them. It is more likely that the true extent of a company's commitment to a policy on discrimination is exemplified by how the company informs its employees. Companies that merely post the printed policy near the time clock, tack it on the bulletin board, or put it in the company handbook or manual are what I call "dead-policy companies." It's not always because these companies don't care about their employees or are disinterested in enforcing such policies. More often, it's about companies not having the resources—specifically time, money, people, and access to authoritative sources—to make a full effort to embrace and support a company position on discrimination. Just the same, the only message these companies are sending to their workers is that they posted a policy, not that they intend to take any measures to enforce it. In these dead-policy companies or those without any visible policy at all, management leaves the search for sources of information to employees, and those sources range from workers gathered around the water cooler to entertainment shows on television.

Statistics indicate that 64 percent of American companies are trying to do something to inform their employees that sexual harassment will not be tolerated. Other statistics indicate that 82 percent of companies need help in doing something. It is a challenge for a company to take on the task of educating its employees on issues of harassment. Although the government sets the guidelines for unlawful sexual harassment, there is often great disparity between the law and the interpretation of the law in the workplace. Many companies are unsure of the methods and communications tools they are using to disseminate information to their employees. There is so much opportunity for interpretation by the company management, by those conducting training, and then by the employees themselves. What seems crystal clear to the government in Washington in regard to sexual harassment issues becomes less clear-cut to a company based in South Dakota or Maine, and the door is opened for interpretation. As a result, there are significant information gaps between the laws on sexual harassment and the people expected to know and practice what the laws preach. It will require the involvement of all affected segments of our society— government agencies, the courts, the business sector, and employees themselves—to close those gaps.

CHAPTER 2

Law and Disorder

Falling into the communication gap

Give to every human being every right that you claim for yourself.

— Robert Ingersoll

THE WINDY CITY CAPER—ELYSSA, PART 1

"I had no intention of getting involved in a lawsuit with my company. I didn't know anything about law. The most legal experience I ever had was trying to get all the parking tickets that I had from parking illegally in front of my apartment building, five times too often, reduced. When my boss tried to sexually assault me, I realized that I didn't know how to handle what had happened to me.

To this day, I can honestly say I never saw it coming. I was friends with all the men I worked with in my department. I suppose we were probably a little arrogant. We made very good money and had a lot of freedom in our jobs. We worked hard, although we did do our share of partying. There were times when I would say we were actually juvenile, pulling stupid tricks on each other, seeing who had the best joke of the day. All of us talked about personal things from time to time. Most of the men I worked with knew when I was dating someone. They would tease me about an "overnight" and say things like they thought I had the same outfit on two days in a row. (Which I didn't.) They loved to hear my stories of "disaster dates," and they would even vote to see whether I should go out with someone again or not.

When I look back, I realize I probably was a little loose about the way I talked about my personal life—but I never talked about sex. My family lived a couple of states away, and I guess I regarded those I worked with as family. Honestly, I thought they were some of the best friends I ever had. Sam, our boss, would always have fun with us, but he knew when to step away from us when he needed to act as our manager. I always felt that I could go to him about anything if I needed to talk about my job or about work in general. I really liked Sam as a person until things started to change.

We were at a sales conference in Chicago and the awards dinner was just ending. Some of the guys had brought their wives, but Sam's wife didn't come, for some reason. Sam asked me if I wanted to go for a drink at the hotel bar. I went, of course, because I considered him a friend and I didn't feel like going back to my room yet. We stayed for about an hour. One minute he was talking about his daughter's riding lessons, and the next minute he told me that I really shouldn't bother with the guys I had been dating. He said that it killed him to hear me talk about other men. He wanted me for himself. He had been in love with me for a long time.

At first, I felt like laughing and was sure he was pulling one off on me. But he seemed serious. Then, I thought he may have had too much to drink so I didn't want to hurt his feelings. I told him I was flattered. He talked about life being short and that we needed to take advantage of every opportunity we have for happiness. He said that he needed to sleep with me. He couldn't hold out anymore. He wanted me that night.

He started to kiss me right in the bar. I got flustered and looked around to see if anyone from the company was in the bar. I had known Sam for four years, and he had never even commented on my hair or clothes like the other guys had. The way he was looking at me that night scared me. I never thought of him as a sexual human being. In fact, even if he wasn't my boss or married, I still wouldn't be interested in him. Not in that way. Never. I rambled on about his being married, but he didn't seem to even hear me. I told him we should go because I wanted to go back to the room and call my best friend. Even if I had to wake her up, I needed to tell her about this.

Sam was staying one floor above me, but he got off at my floor saying he would walk me to my room. I really didn't want him to, but I didn't tell him that. I was already embarrassed about what had happened in the bar. I couldn't wait to get into my room, alone, and shut the door. As I put the key in the door, he started kissing the back of my neck. I squirmed away as I opened the door, but he came right in and lay down on my bed. I told him to leave, saying something that I thought sounded like he would thank me in the morning. But he keep reaching out to me, trying to pull me down on the bed.

He was very persistent, and I started to struggle with him. He started to get violent with me. It happened so fast. He even ripped my pantyhose and the strap of my dress. I finally pushed him back, hard, onto the bed, and grabbed my purse as I left the room. I walked around and around the swimming pool area of the hotel and paced up and down the main hallway for an hour. I couldn't stop crying. I had never seen this coming. I wanted to go talk to Sullivan, one of the other reps, but I was afraid to go to his room. I couldn't imagine what his wife would think of me when she got a look at my torn dress.

Finally, when I went back to my room, he was gone. The next day, we were all meeting for breakfast before we headed to the airport. When I got to the hotel restaurant, Sam was already there. He never looked at me. In fact, he never said a word to me. His face was expressionless, and he just went on talking to Sullivan about a new product announcement. On Monday, back at work, he continued to ignore me. I could hardly function at work. I kept calling my mother, crying, and saying I thought I might move back to Pennsylvania. I guess she thought I was just breaking up with someone and I would pull out of it.

A week passed and I realized Sam wasn't going to bring it up. On Friday, he called me into his office. I thought it was to apologize, but I really felt like it was too late. Instead, he handed me a memo as I walked into his office. It stated that my sales figures were low. He also said he had talked to Dixon, one of my customers, and I had screwed up on delivery arrangements. He was ice cold to me and I honestly didn't know what to say. He dismissed me and told me to go straighten out the problem with the Dixon order.

Every week it was something new, but it was always something I had done wrong. Within a month, my whole job was torn apart. Sam didn't speak to me, I started to be more withdrawn with the other guys I worked with, and I realized that Sam was setting me up to look like I was failing at my job. His manager, Andrew, wasn't in our office; he was based out of Atlanta. Anything Sam told Andrew wouldn't be questioned. If Sam made a recommendation to fire me, it wouldn't be challenged.

I thought about going to human resources, but I didn't know if I could trust anyone there. I never really had much to do with Rachel, the HR director, because the sales department sort of did its own thing. We were the company rebels and, frankly, acted like a lot of the rules didn't apply to us. In fact, there had been a day that sexual harassment sensitivity training had been scheduled, but no one in our department had gone. We thought it was stupid, and one of the guys said he didn't need sexual harassment training, he already knew how to do it. Rachel had scolded us and said we would have to go the next time they had it, but I didn't even know when that was. Of course, the training seminar was before the nightmare in Chicago.

Sam issued a warning to me that my work had to improve.

As incredible as it seemed, I was on some kind of probation. Then, suddenly a new woman, Debbie, had been hired for our department. Sam said she was a sales support person, but I knew what she was going to be. She was going to be my replacement when I was fired. Sam pulled some of my accounts away from me, saying that I really couldn't handle them all. I should focus on making fewer mistakes. I was embarrassed that clients I had worked with for so long were being handled by Debbie. I felt like I was fighting for my life. The guys didn't seem to joke with me anymore. I think they sensed that I was viewed as a weak link by Sam.

It was very lonely. Sam fired me just before Thanksgiving. Rachel was in his office when he called me in and told me they were letting me go. He wanted me to sign a release. I wouldn't. I started to cry and blurted out that I knew it was because of what had happened. When I said that, Rachel just gave Sam a knowing look, like they expected me to come up with some outrageous and false reason for my discharge.

As I look back, I cannot believe that that sales conference in Chicago destroyed my life. Suddenly I was out of work, had lost all contact with my friends from work (even Sullivan blew my calls off), and needed to figure out what to do. I called a friend from the Women in Business Group that I was in (before this, I always thought it was a big waste of time to even go to the meetings) and asked for her help in referring me to a lawyer. I sued my company in federal court for wrongful discharge and sexual harassment. I knew it was going to be a long haul because I hadn't reported it. I still can't believe what prim and proper Sam, the company man, did to me. He changed my life because he wanted to break the rules. I should not have had to pay the price for his behavior."

Elyssa, age 28

UNCIVIL DISOBEDIENCE

Most people don't know it, but sexual harassment in the workplace is a crime. When Congress passed the Civil Rights Act of 1964, as amended, sex discrimination, among other discriminatory acts, became unlawful in the American workplace. In 1980 the Equal Employment Opportunity Commission, the federal agency named to enforce this law, came out with guidelines regarding what kind of behavior constitutes sexual harassment. Back then, though, most workers didn't know who or what the EEOC was, let alone what it might be issuing. So despite the EEOC's good intentions, it was business as usual for most of working America, as we continued to operate as though we hadn't really noticed an official attempt was made to standardize guidelines. At the time, the EEOC was not positioned to hold the kind of press conference that would make the working world stop and listen. Recently, though, the EEOC has developed a very different image. Despite being understaffed, overworked, and buried under a backlog of all kinds of individual discrimination cases, the EEOC has made it clear that it knows how to flex its muscles as the enforcer of discrimination. Today, the agency has emerged as a formidable global power in matters of discrimination and has shown it has the ability to command the immediate attention of any corporation. In fact, it can do it at the drop of a lawsuit, so to speak. In the past few years, the EEOC has been successful in charging a number of corporations with sexual harassment. One case, in fact, led to the biggest settlement in history to date. Contending that over 300 women had been sexually harassed at the auto plant in Normal, Illinois, Mitsubishi Motors Manufacturing of America settled its suit with the EEOC for $34 million.

JUDICIAL EVOLUTION

It isn't just working America that has taken its time comprehending the government's first guidelines. It's been a long and arduous road for courts, judges, and lawyers. It has taken years of court proceedings and case law for the legal definition of sexual harassment to evolve to where it is today. Initially, it took more than ten years from the time the Civil Rights Act of 1964 was enacted for courts to let sexual harassment begin to stand on its own as an employee grievance. After the EEOC guidelines were issued in 1980, the courts struggled through the decade, learning more about the issue with each case that came before the bench. In 1986, the Supreme Court recognized for the first time a sexual harassment complaint in a situation wherein there was no loss of a job or loss of economic benefits. At this time, the Court also added a new standard to the definition of sexual harassment—that the conduct must be unwelcome.

But the nineties have seen the greatest transformation within the legal system with the passage of the Civil Rights Act of 1991. One key provision of the act stipulated that complainants had the right to a jury trial. Another key provision said that compensatory damages, based upon intentional discrimination and unlawful employment practice, and punitive damages, based upon the size of the employer, may be awarded in successful suits. This law opened up great opportunities for redress to those who previously did not have the means or legal support to take on a costly lawsuit. With a record of three decisions on sexual harassment in 1998, the Supreme Court had really spoken out, the media carried the Court's message, and the "victim" felt a power unimaginable in previous decades. Two of those decisions in June 1998 significantly altered sexual harassment law. For the first time the Court really helped out employers by offering clarification about the circumstances in which they would be held liable in sexual harassment cases. It also let out a wake-up call. The High Court made it clear that if employers want to be on the right side of this law, they must take steps to have sound policies prohibiting sexual harassment, effective investigative procedures, and comprehensive training programs for all employees.

The Court's interest and involvement in sexual harassment has increased significantly in the past couple of years, particularly if you track its overall involvement in the past twenty-five years. I suspect that the Court will continue this pace until enough legal guidance has been given to companies so that they adequately manage the tasks within their own companies. Meanwhile, though, I believe it will be a bumpy road, blocked here and there with various obstacles having to do with other types of constitutional and corporate rights.

From my experience in educating companies and organizations, I have learned that most people know little about the roots of the civil rights law and frankly have expressed little interest in learning more. If participants' eyelids are going to get heavy during a workplace seminar on sensitivity, it's undoubtedly going to be during the section on law. Having observed that, I still believe it is extremely important that we understand that there is a legal basis for the definition of sexual behavior at work. In employee group discussions, someone is always quick to say that Gloria Steinem, or Betty Friedan, or even Anita Hill, is behind some "feminist movement deal" plotting to destroy sex lives. From what I know of Steinem, Friedan, or Hill, I suspect they would be flattered that someone thought they had the sheer power and ability to mobilize females in such a global *Star Wars* kind of operation to zap out sex in our lifetime (even though zapping out sex was never their goal). But they are not the force behind the law. Despite dissenters, the law regarding sexual harassment has had a life all its own, propelled by its own power. And remember, it isn't sex that Congress was trying to regulate back in 1964—it was discrimination *because* of sex/gender.

GOING PUBLIC

If you went out and asked people on the street when they think sexual harassment became a problem in the workplace, one response might be to tell you that harassment noticeably became an issue when women, with a steady frequency, began to complain about it. While such a response seems unenlightened, there is some truth to it. For the business community, harassment became a serious issue when the claims took on financial implications, in terms of damaging a company's reputation. Once the issue caught the eye of an interested public, cases didn't need to wait to be tried in court. The public exposure allowed claims to take a different course in a way that upped the stakes for both sides. Beginning in the early nineties, the media began to describe case after case of legal face-offs between employee and employer, revealing scandalous details of sexual misconduct along the way. Those charged seemed irresponsible; the companies they worked for, perhaps liable. The burden of the crisis began to shift to companies. If companies fought a complainant openly, they would look coldhearted. If they remained completely silent, they would appear guilty. Suddenly, businesses had a challenge on their hands that required not only legal expertise and dexterity in crisis deactivation skills, but a companywide showing of sensitivity as well.

Knowing that all this is going on, you would think we'd make it our business to have a better grasp of the specific kinds of sexual behavior that are actually against the law. Regardless of our sense of right and wrong, if only for purposes of basic self-protection it would seem we would be motivated to understand where the lines of distinction are drawn. That way, we could simply take sexual harassment from its murky state and confidently flip it over to the black-and-white list of what are wrongful acts in our society. On that list, of course, would already be the usual violations ranging from auto theft to Lizzie Borden stuff; and now sexual harassment in the workplace would take its rightful place. If it was clear, most of us would make more of an effort to abide by society's recommendations, or at least think twice before we got involved in something inappropriate at work. But many have trouble getting to that point. How can human behavior that seems so "normal" under different circumstances be considered wrong when it happens between people who work together? After all, some say, men and women, sexual attraction, social interaction—these should hardly be regulated by civil laws. More vocal protesters claim that not only are we violating privacy rights, but we are sterilizing our world at work—heading straight toward an emotionless workplace, devoid of any signs of human life. But the purpose of the law is not to separate the sexes, but to protect men and women from an issue that threatens to unfairly separate men and women.

SEXUAL MISCONDUCT: THE EFFECTS OF FALLOUT

The focus of this book is on sexual harassment in the workplace. It is not about Washington politics or the office of the presidency or the future of the internship program at the White House. But, certainly, it is about fallout, specifically the far-reaching kind that affects everyone and everything that may have any reason to be exposed. In the case of the president of the United States being sued by a former employee for sexual harassment, we are talking about tremendous global fallout. The settlement came far too late to save the president or the people around him from the maximum impact caused by these cases. Paula Jones's claim against President Clinton (alleged to have taken place when he was governor of Arkansas) triggered the biggest and most visible chain of events ever to occur following a public claim of sexual misconduct. The events that occurred as a result of this claim are something we need to take a closer look at, particularly as we consider the impact of sexual harassment in all workplaces. Forgetting politics and motivations and who's good and who's evil, what happened *after* is what is most important in this case. There are vital lessons for corporate America to learn from President Clinton's experiences in being sued for sexual harassment. Whether or not the charges are true, the impact of sexual harassment charges on an organization, an individual, and, in this case, an entire global community are sharply clear.

The charges against President Clinton kicked up a storm of debate on specific aspects of sexual harassment. For example, if such behavior took place, what needs to occur to make a complainant feel wronged? Is there a time line for sexual harassment? What combination of events needs to happen to qualify as "harassment" and be serious enough to actually injure a worker? And what *is* an injury in a sexual harassment case? Does it mean the person is physically ill from the experience, or does the term *injury* include the breaking of a person's spirit and the loss of all professional drive? Is the manipulative act of a superior putting a worker in that position enough of an inappropriate deed to wrong an employee?

Although there are various cases that have directly and indirectly addressed the frequency and severity of sexual harassment, there is still great confusion about how many "hits" must take place for it to be real harassment and not just offensive behavior. Many people are just champing at the bit in their search for a simple mathematical formula. (OK, you were kissed at the office, that's two points.) But the issue defies such simple-minded quantification. I heard several "talking heads" on television discussing the alleged fifteen minutes in a hotel room where the boss was asking for oral sex. To these commentators, the central issue was how much time had passed, not the sexual request! Flashers on the street work at lightning speed, but we know what they've done and we know it's wrong. Just because harassment may happen only once, or for a short amount of time, doesn't mean it's not serious harassment. There is no other wrongful behavior to which we apply such conditions.

The allegations against Clinton weren't the first time I had heard of such a scenario. Once a woman came to me who was on the verge of collapse. She worked for the head of a religious organization in the New York area. One night, the director, who was also a rabbi, pulled his pants down in his office and pushed her over the credenza behind his desk. He, too, requested oral sex. When she went to the others in the organization looking for help, they shunned her. She was immediately fired, and her personnel file instantly contained several documents that referred to her emotionally unstable state. She was portrayed as delusional. No one would take her case. No one would go near her. The power of the organization and the ranking of the executive director in the community made her a "nothing." Another woman, back in 1987, came to me with a similar story. A high-ranking county official, from a beloved local family, made it a practice to unzip his pants and point to his crotch when she walked into his office at the end of the day. She experienced the same problem as the woman in New York. He was from a powerful family who ruled in that local kingdom. Both these women were emotionally distraught from these experiences, and they underwent the same difficulties in starting over. They had no justice, they lost their jobs, and they were left with terrible memories of what they both termed "a dirty, horrible experience."

Even though the courts are working at producing case law that helps to further define sexual harassment, it still is a case-by-case approach to understanding where the line is between merely obnoxious and annoying behavior and that which is against the law. It has occurred to me that perhaps some people don't have an interest in finding out where the line is drawn because it is easier to get away with wrongdoing if you don't know the boundaries. Ignorance is bliss, and it is also, in the case of harassment, remissness.

FOLLOW THE LEADER?

Our very separate roles as professional working people and sexual human beings often don't stay separate, and ultimately become one and the same, sometimes with enormous consequences. Sexual misconduct in the workplace isn't just about President Clinton—it's about all of us. The embarrassing public exposure of his alleged sexual trysts, trials, and tribulations should serve as an example to corporate America of what a sex scandal can do to a work environment. When an internal charge of sexual harassment hits the light of day and becomes a lawsuit, even the average person finds everything around him or her in jeopardy. When a legal action hits a chief executive officer, it is a mammoth problem that needs around-the-clock skilled care. It becomes everyone's problem. If we look at Mr. Clinton's ordeal as simply a CEO in legal trouble, it can provide all of us with an incredible lesson of what could happen to our own companies, our own lives, if sexual misconduct goes unchecked.

HE SAID, SHE SAID, THEY SAID, AND WE SAID

If President Clinton really were just "John Doe the CEO," the chain of events leading to that lawsuit would go something like this:

- A woman claims that the CEO of her company has requested oral sex from her while she is attending a trade show. She turns him down. No one else was in the room at the time, SHE SAID.

- He never did it, HE SAID.

- She feels what she experienced was sexual harassment and that it adversely affected her. With help from special-interest groups, she goes outside the company and finds lawyers to represent her. Her lawyers look for a pattern—had John Doe the CEO ever done anything like this before? Is he still doing it? The lawyers look and they find. There may be a pattern of requesting sex from employees. People need to be brought in to support this "pattern and practice" legal strategy.

- The company has a policy on sexual harassment which the company holds everyone responsible for upholding—but *this* is the CEO—do the same rules apply to him?

- A few board members decide on behalf of the company that the same standards don't apply to their CEO. The director of HR is furious with senior management because she has been told to soft-pedal the charge of sexual harassment. If it were anyone else, they said, she could handle matters in the standard way, but this wasn't just any employee. She feels as if she has lost all her credibility with other employees that she has worked with to resolve complaints in the past.

- People do get pulled into the legal battle. Some are still working for the company, others have left. Those that work for John Doe, are nervous that somehow they are now involved, and they don't want to be. They feel torn between their loyalty to their CEO and their concern for their own jobs, and anxious about having to compromise their own ethics for the sake of their boss.

- The CEO's executive secretary is put through the legal wringer. She is asked for all kinds of records and calendars. She is drilled by the company's attorneys. They need to know what she knows in order to properly assess the situation. She can hardly show up for work these days. Frankly, her respect for her boss is waning. She's no longer making eye contact with him.

- Employees start talking to each other and to the outside community.

- Members of the press, knowing that legal papers have been filed, begin following the story, from the inside out. They start parking outside the company's gate. They are stationed outside the CEO's home. Employees leaving work for the day answer questions that the media ask. Other employees avoid the press. Those who are willing to talk to the press and those who aren't start turning against each other.

- The public relations department of the company doesn't know what it should say when reporters call and ask for comment. The staff members in the department haven't heard from the corporation's counsel because the counsel have been meeting with the CEO's private attorneys for three days. Then they find out that the CEO's private attorneys have made a comment to the press that isn't like anything the company would have allowed under normal circumstances. Employees call. They are upset. Why doesn't anyone in the company tell them what is going on? The public relations staff can't tell employees because they don't know what is going on, either.

- The woman charging the CEO with sexual harassment has an unscheduled press conference. She appears on television with members of special-interest groups by her side, including representatives from the National Organization for Women.

- Now, the board of directors starts to become concerned. Board members have always counted on the CEO to keep them informed of internal matters. The CEO always protected them from the enemy. It is starting to feel like *he* might be it, under these circumstances. They don't know how to handle this one. Communication breaks down. They start wondering about their own liability. The company's stock price has dipped. Is it coincidence or is it connected?

- The company's lawyers are working night and day to defend the CEO and the company. The legal bills are headed skyward, but there is no choice.

- Special-interest groups are boycotting the company's product. No one in the company has a readied plan to address the boycott. Distributors are calling and are furious. Retailers are upset because it is their stores that are being picketed. The marketing department calls the public relations department asking that someone stop the boycott. About 52 percent of the company's products are sold to women. The company can't afford to have members of NOW appear on television with the former employee suing the CEO.

- John Doe the CEO remains at his job, but he is always tied up with private meetings with the lawyers. His time is consumed with defending himself against the charges of sexual harassment. The chairman of the board has called and would like the number two person to run the company for a while, at least until this is over. He asks the CEO to pretend he is still in command, but in reality, he is not. In fact, he may never be again. The chairman asks the CEO to do everything he personally can to get this thing behind him, and the company. Both know the company is in crisis, and no one there has even taken a deposition yet.

LEARNING CURVES—ELYSSA, PART 2

Although what happened to Elyssa was not her fault, her case shows some of the problems that result from being unprepared for an incident and, of equal importance, being unaware of the law. What Sam did was a form of sexual harassment called *quid pro quo*. In this case, it was also criminal, as it was a sexual assault and attempted rape. He wanted to have sex with his employee. When she refused, he tried to force himself upon her. Afterward, he retaliated against her professionally and carried out a strategy that would allow him to fire her. Only he (and Elyssa) would know that his reasons were pretextual. This is the most common type of reaction when a superior is rebuffed by a subordinate. The superior wants the sexual harassment target out of the organization.

Because Elyssa never reported the incident to the hotel, to the organization sponsoring the event, to her company's human resources department, or to Andrew, Sam's boss, she would later have a difficult time proving that the assault actually occurred. Up until the time she attended the award conference, she had a good employment record. But once Sam had time to create the impression of her as a poor employee, he had enough ammunition to substantiate firing her. When this kind of retaliation occurs, employees feel powerless. When supervisors are able to change an employee's standing, internal reputation, and performance rating within a short period of time, they are showing even more power than they may have when they made their sexual advances.

When I investigate an alleged quid pro quo, I look for sudden changes in a person's performance. There are often two reasons for such changes, and they are closely related: The person's supervisor may be setting the person up, *and* the impact of the incident may be creating such a hostile environment for the person that it hurts his or her morale, productivity, and quality of work. What the person is going through—psychologically and professionally—starts to show. Of course, another possibility is that the claim is false. If a review of performance over a longer period of time is available, showing a history of poor performance long before an alleged incident occurred, the claim may be a way a worker wants to seek protection from being fired.

Elyssa also made the mistake of thinking that she was immune to the problem of sexual harassment. She worked at being "one of the guys" during her employment with the company. She was only accepted as one of them when she didn't experience any discrimination, especially the kind that women most often experience. When the men in her department sensed that Elyssa was falling out of favor with Sam, their survival instincts told them to pull away. As a member of the team, she was losing her power. She was acting strangely, besides—very moody and withdrawn. She probably got shot down by some guy and was getting bored with her work, Sullivan had thought. It seemed that her department only wanted to be friends with her when she was successful and secure in her role within the department. Elyssa didn't realize that the bonds between the men in the department were stronger than the friendships that she had with her coworkers. When Elyssa was first fired, one of the guys even complimented Sam for having the courage to get rid of a nonperformer. Elyssa's former coworker told Sam he thought it was a tough and gutsy move and he admired his management style. Of course, he thought Elyssa was a lot of fun, a sweet kid, really, but he knew Sam was just doing what he had to do for the sake of the department's billing.

Elyssa also made the mistake of disregarding the company's educational efforts on sexual harassment. She hadn't attended the sexual harassment seminar and didn't know what she should do to report sexual harassment at her company. She also sent a message to her coworkers that the issue wasn't important to her. At least, at the time it wasn't.

When Elyssa first sued her company, her case started out looking very weak. But at closer examination, her case found substance in Sam's post-Chicago behavior. Sam did have holes in his postincident plan of showing a paper trail of Elyssa's work performance declining. Sam had been overactive in seeking out criticism of Elyssa from her customers. In fact, her customers, when subpoenaed, admitted that they had never heard from Sam before; in fact, it was only during those two months after Elyssa's assault that Sam made any direct contact with them. They felt it odd that Sam was calling them and searching for something Elyssa may have failed to do. Someone that worked at the desk of the hotel had seen Elyssa the night she walked into the lobby after the incident and was prepared to tell a jury that Elyssa's dress was ripped, and she was visibly shaken. In fact, the desk clerk had asked someone to take over for her to go find the woman, but she had disappeared.

In this case, no one saw the assault; it never occurred again. There was no sexual advances prior to the assault and her boss had never shown her the least bit of disrespect for her as a woman or as a person prior to that night. That's why quid pro quo sexual harassment has been termed a silent offender. *No one sees it, but it happens.*

The company settled the case for an undisclosed amount of money, but not because they thought Sam did it. They only wanted to end something distasteful before it became public. Elyssa was ordered to sign a release and a confidentiality agreement, which restricted her from ever discussing the case or the terms of the agreement. She remains upset, despite the settlement, and has had a great deal of trouble moving on with her life. She is no longer interested in the same field and cannot find one that is as fulfilling. Her biggest concern is that Sam got away with it and her life was never put back together. She knows that everyone in the community still thinks highly of him, and he hasn't lost any of his standing, either professionally or personally. Recently, she saw Sam's wife's picture in the paper for heading up a charity fund-raiser for abused women. Justice, she told me, was not anything she really concerned herself with, until she realized it was something she was never going to be able to claim. Now, it haunts her daily.

CHAPTER 3

Going Behind Power Zones

Understanding motive and opportunity

I know, up on top
you are seeing great sights,
But down at the bottom
we, too, should have rights.

—Dr. Seuss

Yertle the Turtle and Other Stories

(New York, Random House, 1997)

DOWN AT THE BOTTOM

After a speech I gave at a university, a male student asked if he could speak with me privately. Mark was an engineering student and was just finishing his fifth year of studies. He had participated in a co-op program through the university and had worked every other semester at a large corporation. He had found his way into a particular company because it was where he wanted to work after graduation. He had received superior evaluations from his various supervisors and recently accepted a permanent job with the company.

On the surface, his future looked great. His problem now, he told me, was one that he didn't know how to deal with, and he was afraid it could cost him his future. His new supervisor was a woman that he hadn't worked with previously. Within the past few months, as he finished out his last co-op semester, he had been assigned to work under Cynthia. Cynthia was unmarried and about eight years older than Mark. She was making it very clear, in a number of ways, that she wanted to be involved with him sexually.

At first, Mark wasn't sure what was happening. Cynthia would tell him there was an event that he should attend, something that she thought would be good for his career. She would make all the arrangements for him to attend. When he did, she went with him, "like a date." Recently, she was forcing him to play tennis with her, have lunch and dinner with her, and do activities with her that had nothing at all to do with his work. Now, she was starting to make comments about his looks and his youthful virility. She had come on to him more than once. When he got flustered, she told him how cute and innocent he was. She told him it made him even more attractive.

He hadn't told his girlfriend about Cynthia's overtures because he was afraid she might think that he was responsible for them. (After all, he *was* the guy, he told me.) Mark wanted to tell someone else at work about it, but knew that Cynthia was one of the more senior women in engineering. Because she was one of the few female executives in the company, she had a great deal of power. He felt that if she ever found out he complained to anyone, she would have him tossed out of the company in a blink of the eye. "I'm twenty-one, and I've worked hard to get into this position," stated Mark. "How can she do this to me at the beginning of my career? I'm embarrassed that it is happening to me, but I am also very, very angry that she is using the power she has over me for her own personal reasons. How can I request a transfer when I just started full-time? And if I leave after a few months and go somewhere else, what does that look like on my resume? This is a horrible deal, and I didn't ask for any of it."

POWERFUL PEOPLE IN POWERFUL PLACES
"OH, IT'S GOOD TO BE KING."

This is a line from a Mel Brooks movie that always crosses my mind when I see a larger-than-life powerful figure, a Donald Trump type, announcing that he is going to change the time zones to suit his frantic schedule or going to buy up Manhattan Island instead of Roosevelt Island because it has more fashion models per square block. In America, it really is good to be king. Powerful people don't make small moves— they make *power moves*. And (it seems) we like to watch them make their moves, even if we don't particularly like what they are doing— morally, ethically, socially, or otherwise. They themselves aren't nearly as interesting as the power we believe they possess. Even world leader Henry Kissinger once said that power was the ultimate aphrodisiac. Whatever it is about power, we want to know more about it so that, just maybe, we can have some of it work its way into our lives.

Following the lives of omnipotent people has long been an obsession for many of us around the world. We watch these influential figures live. And when they die, well, we watch that too. The power a person once possessed in life doesn't turn to ashes when the person dies. When a current-day legend has passed on, we just begin to watch those who were once close to him or her to see what *they* are doing. We make lists of the "most powerful," the "sexiest," and the "richest." Our fixation on the high-potency ruling class of our day is probably based upon a strange mix of admiration, captivation, envy, and the search for a thread of connection to these people. Power as an entity is interwoven into the core of our culture.

POWER RANGERS

Powerful people attract us even if they don't have all the physical, intellectual, or spiritual attributes we expect or hope for in "regular people" that we admire. As a society we overlook their flaws, including personality and behavioral shortcomings. We forgive these power gods and goddesses because we don't want to do anything to tamper with, or lessen, *the power* found inside the vessel. We will look past, if we must, and we will pardon almost anything. Those who are in positions of authority, and who are in the position to be examples, even role models, can screw up royally. Yet we do not castigate them the way we would our neighbor, spouse, or local business leader. However, most recently, some are taking issue with this American practice of forgive and forget. In his 1998 book, *Death of Outrage* (New York, The Free Press, 1998), former Secretary of Education William J. Bennett spoke out against the trend to disregard irresponsible behavior, especially irresponsible sexual behavior:

> In much of modern America, there seems to be a belief that anything that involves sex is, or ought to be, forgotten; here we

see a River Lethe effect permeating our culture. In Greek mythology, Lethe is one of the rivers of Hades. The souls of the dead are obliged to taste its water, so that they may forget everything said and done while alive. Today, many Americans feel we should drink the water and forget. The sentiment is: One should simply respond to sexual misconduct with that watchword of our time, "Whatever." Sex becomes a No Accountability Zone.

POWERFUL BEGINNINGS

How we perceive, use, and misuse power can be traced back to our childhood. Think back to the books our parents and teachers read to us. The really gutsy fables and tales were about power. Personally, I remember power and the imbalance of power being a story line in almost all the stories that touched my own life. Being king of the jungle and having power was a *huge* deal. If the heros or heroines weren't kings or queens, chances are they had special skills, abilities, or talents that were going to help make them be "the finest in all the land" pretty darn quick. When we heard stories about "the oppressed," or those without power, we cheered them on in their struggles to get power—which they did, by the way. If there were any stories about wimps, frankly we weren't all that interested.

And, of course, in classic stories, the lack of power in the roles women were given has always concerned feminists. Many of the "girls" like Snow White and Cinderella had very little power of their own and were looking for—*or falling for*—guys with power. In *Bearing Witness,* Celia Morris contends that familiar stories such as these shaped women and influenced the way that women would be viewed in their lifetime. Using Peter Rabbit's tale of a "grand adventure in Farmer McGregor's garden," Morris points out that Peter had the powerful experience while his sisters Flopsy, Mopsy, and Cotton-tail, like good bunnies, cowered at home. Morris believes that stories like this one are "embedded in our culture, implicitly teaching boys to live a certain way and girls to live another." Carolyn Heilbrun takes the idea of power in storytelling far beyond classic fairy tales. In her book, *Writing a Woman's Life*, she states that "power consists to a large extent in deciding what stories will be told [in history,] [and] male power has made certain stories unthinkable." In other words, history itself has been recorded and interpreted largely by men. Ten years later, we are certainly showing signs that male and female opportunities for storytelling are equalizing out. In fact, the current and popular ABC television talk show aptly entitled *The View* is proof that women's views of issues and events are not only showcased, but encouraged.

My early education on power was from both books and four brothers. I grew up as the only girl in a house of boys. Clearly by starting out my life in a male-dominated environment I was given an early opportunity to understand that power is something that is not evenly distributed between the two genders. To me, there was a certain advantage to being close enough to watch how the world, back then, treated males differently from females. I wouldn't have traded my sibling mix for the world, because it helped me figure out how to get my own vote counted and my own voice heard. It's part of what I am today. This is why we have to recognize in the workplace that people really bring all their past—their childhood, their experiences in former jobs, their education, their social and political views—into the workplace with them.

SEXUAL POWER

In the movie *Working Girl*, Melanie Griffith's character said, "She had a mind for business and a bod for sin." Many working men assert that women flaunt their sexuality in the workplace. Those men are right. Some women definitely "work the workplace," and they are very comfortable with their choice.

Several male employees have told me that *they just know* women read magazines that tell them how to "catch guys' interests" at work. "You know, they learn how to slowly cross and uncross their legs at work, what to wear, how to move their lips sensually in meetings. They are being trained to attract men in the workplace, and we fall for it. Then we get sued."

That's a little dramatic, but there is also some truth to be found here regarding the mixed messages currently bouncing off cubicle partitions and office walls in the workplace. Some women *are* looking for husbands. Some, quite matter-of-factly, admit that they are merely searching the office directory for nothing more than a "good time." And some, unfortunately, are looking for a way to use their sexuality to obtain better jobs and better opportunities. A study released in late 1998 reported that there are women who openly admit that they want the opportunity to sleep their way to the top of their organization. Not surprisingly, working women are sharply divided over this kind of behavior. Staunchly defending it, one former talk show commentator (MTV generation representative) said that women should be able to use their sexuality in the workplace to their own personal advantage. It levels the playing field that was originally built for men inside the arena known as "a man's world." After all, said the twenty-something woman, "My sexuality is my power, and I am going to use everything I've got. That's what I believe I am supposed to *use it* for."

THE POWER BETWEEN THE SEXES

Men and women communicate very differently say today's top experts on the topic. Thanks to relationship communication experts like John Gray and Deborah Tannen, we are getting a clearer grasp on this concept. Deborah Tannen, in her book *You Just Don't Understand,* states that many men are culturally conditioned to see communication as asymmetrical, in which one person has more power or superiority over the other. Tannen believes that women often seek symmetry in a relationship and that they reinforce the ways in which both people are the

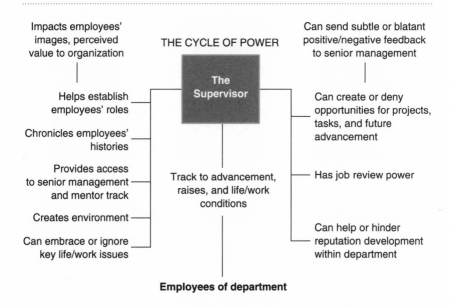

Impacts employees' images, perceived value to organization

THE CYCLE OF POWER

Can send subtle or blatant positive/negative feedback to senior management

The Supervisor

Helps establish employees' roles

Can create or deny opportunities for projects, tasks, and future advancement

Chronicles employees' histories

Provides access to senior management and mentor track

Track to advancement, raises, and life/work conditions

Has job review power

Creates environment

Can embrace or ignore key life/work issues

Can help or hinder reputation development within department

Employees of department

same or equal. So women may be particularly sensitive to feeling put down by men. It feels like a power move.

New York City psychologist Marion Gindes, a specialist in workplace sexual harassment, asserts that many men and women sexualize their working relationships because it is the way in which they feel comfortable relating to each other. They really don't know any other way to treat the other sex. It's the way they did it growing up, and it's the way they behave at home.

Just a couple of years ago, I was in a meeting with a general manager of a company. The general manager had his shoes off and was playing footsie with his secretary, who was sitting next to me. The secretary seemed totally devoted to her married boss and would do any task he requested of her. She shopped for him, worked for him, took care of him. She appeared to believe that he was a powerful figure in the company, but she had her own power. She could take care of him better than anyone else, including other staff members and even his wife. In fact, she wanted to take care of him much better than his wife did. She enjoyed showing her up.

Gindes recalls one case where a woman went to bed with her foreman because she thought it was expected. In the past, at her place of business, it had been the norm. It was just the way things were done in that working environment.

Gindes also notes that some "seasoned working women" object to the elimination of sizzling sex sparks between men and women in the workplace. In fact, some women feel that it is dead wrong to take the sex out of the workplace. One woman commented that men and women are about sex. She said, "We are beyond the point where we need to be concerned about whether women can do the job. They can. So let the sexual attraction and tension between men and women stay. It keeps the workplace exciting and all of us can always use a little excitement."

Gindes has observed that this type of woman also believes that she made her own way through the workplace and up the ladder. She is disinterested in helping out a freshman class of raving feminists. This type of woman believes that each woman needs to pay her dues, just like she had to do. Why should other women have it any easier?

BOSS POWER AND OTHER POWER

If a company doesn't provide checks and balances to protect all employees from the abuse of power, those we report to, those above us, can pull the strings of authority at whim. If the power of an organization lies in the hands of individuals and is not found within the structure or foundation of a company, every single employee is vulnerable to the misuse of power. Most victims of sexual misconduct are most stunned by the force of power when they have rejected a superior, or even complained in an environment where claims are not wanted. The power that is abused in cases of sexual harassment is often the same power that is used to rid an employee that rebuffs a superiors sexual advances.

THE POWER OF THE CEO

If a CEO believes in the importance of ethics and fairness:

If a CEO does not place any importance on diversity, ethics, and zero tolerance for sexual harassment:

CEO

CEO drives his/her beliefs/regard on values/ethics and commitment to high standards through both mission statement and daily leadership.

CEO sends that message to senior management and employees through noncommunication.

Senior and middle management follows lead from CEO and contributes own initiatives within because they know ideas will be welcome.

Senior management acts or fails to act independently and minimizes employees' needs and concerns.

Employees feel devalued and individually worthless to the organization.

Personal power of employees is strengthened by clear communication from CEO that corporate ethics exists in all areas of company.

TOP-DOWN POWER FLOW THROUGH THE ORGANIZATION

Employees *trust* their organization and feel that their complaints will be handled fairly.

POWER TOOLS

As the definition of sexual harassment has been debated, expert opinions on what fuels the engine that moves sexual harassment through the workplace have generalized it with the now often used expression that "sexual harassment isn't about sex as much as it is about power." Sexual harassment *is* often about power, because power is often necessary to carry out the control aspects associated with sexual harassment. But I do believe that in certain cases it is also about sex. In situations where a superior is controlling a "weaker" subordinate, sex can be the tool. In other cases, where a superior or a coworker is deeply attracted to, maybe even obsessed with, another person, sex is the goal.

In "hostile work environments" sex is not the goal but the culture.

When even a few employees are permitted to openly engage in sexual expression, specifically sexual speech, it often is at the expense of someone they work with. This is the point at which critics of the parameters of Title VII become vocal about the First Amendment. Hans Bader, an attorney at the Center for Individual Rights in Washington, D.C., in an 1997 *National Law Journal* article wrote, "In theory, harassment law only restricts speech that is 'severe or pervasive' enough to alter the work environment. But this standard is very vague, since 'one person's discussion may be another person's harassment.' "

POWER MOVES

Here are some of the ways in which supervisors can exert power over us:

- They can direct and indirectly shape the image that others have of us.

- They can give us opportunities, specific projects, that others won't have the chance to work on, but will give us a chance to work with someone or on something that is both enjoyable and good for our career.

- They can speak for us, and about us, to their superiors. This can affect our future and determine whether or not we have the respect of management and are perceived as valuable.

- Through their actions they can show coworkers how they regard us. Coworkers show more respect for highly regarded employees.

- They can in subtle or overt ways determine the style and way in which we work.

The power spread within an organization includes employees as well as bosses but with dramatic degrees and weight. Elissa Perry, Ph.D., a professor of organizational behavior and theory at Teachers College, Columbia University, says the key to whether or not an employee can report sexual harassment is whether or not that employee is perceived as having personal power. The personal power the employee has individually and as part of the organization will probably affect (whether the company admits it or not) how seriously the organization takes the employee's claim. Dr. Perry also notes that the personal power felt by employees is based upon their feelings or perception about their company's ethnicity. Employees feel empowered personally when they work for a company that has created an environment based upon high standards, sound corporate ethics, and good communication.

Beginning with the earliest accounts of sexual harassment told by domestic help who feared for their lives if they rejected their "masters" to present settings complete with the latest high-tech harassment methods, the study of the abuse of power in the workplace has shown consistency in form and practice. What is also interesting in this closer examination of motive and opportunity is that profiles of individuals actually seem to develop. Over the past fifteen years, I have noted similarities in the individuals who engage in this type of sexual abuse, and have actually been able to group these individuals into "profiles."

CHAPTER 4

Who's Who in Sexual Harassment

Identifying offenders, pretenders, and serious rule-benders

Everybody is who he was in high school.

—Calvin Trillin

The 2,548 Best Things Anybody Ever Said,

Ed. Robert Byrne

(New York, Galahad Books, 1996)

"**D**iana and I were involved for about 2½ years. At the time, I really thought I knew her. We worked for one of the largest banks in the world and didn't meet until I had been asked to run the regional branch of the Philadelphia division. Diana is very smart and extremely competent. It was a dream to have that kind of support in my new position. She brought me up to speed on the internal politics, and offered good advice on how to handle some of the ruffled feathers of those who wanted my position and didn't get it. She also was invaluable in helping me find my way through a rather "cliquey" business community. She took care of all of that so that I could concentrate on the real work before me.

I really liked her, so it seemed natural when one thing led to another. When we became involved sexually, I thought we both knew its limitations. I was already married for the second time, and had no interest in going through another divorce. I didn't have the strength for it. Diana seemed very happy that I was only partly available. She always told me she wasn't interested in a full-time husband. Her work was demanding, and she didn't feel that "playing the wife" was anything she was interested in doing at that point in her life.

We were very discreet and never let anyone at work know about our affair. The only time we had a problem was when Diana went ballistic on me for giving her what she called a "lousy review." I had explained to her that I gave her a good review but not a glowing one to protect our relationship. I didn't want anyone to suspect I was showing favoritism. She was angry with me, but she got past it once she understood why I had handled it the way I did.

After I had been in the regional president position for three years, I was asked to take a position in New Jersey. It was a big promotion for me. I couldn't even think of passing it up. I didn't take Diana with me. I couldn't. She seemed to understand at first, but her phone calls started to get very needy once I made the move. She hated her new boss, and he was coming down hard on her.

She showed up in my new office one day, and it turned into a terrible scene. I told her I didn't want to continue our affair. I couldn't handle it anymore. She was telling me that my official reviews of her had adversely impacted her career at the bank. Her new boss wanted someone else in her position. She was being demoted. I calmed her down and finally got her to leave.

Following that meeting, she called several times a day for weeks. She was leaving all sorts of e-mails for me. Those shook me up, because I couldn't let my secretary see them, and I didn't have time to monitor my own e-mail. But Diana's e-mails forced me to spend time throughout the day checking to make sure she hadn't left one. Once, she sent a letter to my home. Fortunately, I, and not my wife, was the one who happened to pull it out of the mailbox.

Then, suddenly, all the telephone calls, e-mails, and letters stopped. I was so relieved until Wayne, my boss from New York, called me and said he needed to talk to me about a serious matter. I went to New York to meet with him. As soon as I sat down with him and saw Diana's return address on the letter he was holding, I knew I was moments away from losing everything. I thought I would stop breathing.

Wayne told me what her letter said. She knew enough to contact him directly, although she had also gone to the head of human resources. She was accusing me of sexual harassment. My life flashed before my eyes. I thought of my new job, my wife, my kids, my future with the bank. All of it was being blown apart, and Diana had the power to do it.

I would give anything to turn back time so that I could have passed up the affair. Frankly, after it was over, I realized my relationship with my wife was a good one. I was so sorry I had jeopardized it. I also think I would have done just fine in that position in Philadelphia without Diana's support. She wanted me to think she was invaluable and therefore indebted. I realize, now, it was her way to pull me closer. I don't know what I was thinking of, but I can't believe the price I am now going to have to pay."

Robert, age 44

IDENTIFYING HARASSERS

One of the most frequent questions I am asked by management regarding sexual harassment is what is the typical harasser like. Understandably, management is looking for the profile that depicts what kind of men are doing the harassing. After all, if we had specific profiles of whom to look out for, it would certainly make the job of managing much easier. Early flashing warning signs that identify employees who are going to cause trouble in the area of discrimination would mean that you could head them off at the pass. But there are some indications that the "invisible stuff" we carry with us into the workplace, rather than the "visible stuff," affects how we treat each other.

Psychologists say that much of what constitutes sexual harassment behavior is so much about a person's beliefs, attitudes, and sexual education. The longer I am in this area of work, the more I believe that people behave in the workplace much like they behaved as a child in school and at home. So kindergarten rules like keep your hands to yourself, respect others, don't taunt, play fair, don't gross out the other kids on the playground, could almost be reassembled with bigger, more

---

ABOUT VICTIMS OF SEXUAL HARASSMENT*

Most victims are women.

Ninety percent of incident reports are made by women.

Female victims are younger than the average age of the general female population. Usually female victims are in their twenties or thirties. Specifically women who are subject to severe forms of harassment are between twenty-four and thirty-four.

Women who are married or widowed are less likely to be harassed than women who are divorced, are separated, or have never married.

Over 40 percent of complainants are high school graduates, slightly over 50 percent have some college experience, 13 percent have some college experience, and 38 percent have graduated from college.

Being in a job that is traditionally performed by just one sex also seems to make experiences more likely.

*David E. Terpstra, "Who Gets Sexually Harassed?" *Personnel Administrator* (March 1989), pp. 84–88, 111. US Merit Protection Board Study, supra note 1. "Sexual Harassment in the Workplace," Ellen Wagner, pp. 7–8.

---

formal-sounding words and made into the rules for today's workplace. Instead of saying keep your hands to yourself, we could say to working people, "While interacting with either gender in the workplace, it is best to refrain from any kind of unwanted physical contact."

As incredible as it sounds, in my consulting practice I have had to have serious discussions with executives of multimillion-dollar companies regarding antics that have occurred between people who make in excess of $100,000 a year. They have been disciplined by their employers for pulling their pants down and "mooning" employees at corporate outings, for wearing ties with a penis displayed on it for casual dress day,

ABOUT HARASSERS*

Usually harassers are male, older than their victims, married, and considered unattractive by the victims.

Numerically, most harassers are coworkers, but the most frequently reported harassment is from supervisors to subordinates.

Harassers frequently bother more than one person, and the incidents reoccur over an extended period of time.

The higher the percentage of men in the workplace, the more harassment of women occurs.

Motivations generally fall into three categories (according to studies of men):

- Actual sexual desire
- Personal power (by harassment the man makes himself feel more important, virile)
- Social control (the man who does not like women in the workplace environment harasses to get rid of them or to put them in their place)

Most men do not sexually harass. One estimate is that only 5 percent of men are even capable of such behavior.

Female harassers are involved in an estimated 1 percent of cases. Their victims are almost always men; homosexual female harassment is rare.

Female harassers are usually divorced or single and are younger than their victims.

The "average" man who propositions or harasses a woman is much like the "average" man in the workforce. The "average" woman who makes advances is not at all typical of the "average" woman, and is likely to be a supervisor.

*Susan L. Webb, *Step Forward: Sexual Harassment in the Workplace— What You Need to Know!* (Mastermedia Ltd, New York, 1991), pp. 63–64.

for having sex in the ladies room, for showing porn films as a prank to open up the sales meeting, for putting jock straps on female employees' desks, for drawing breasts on the photographs of the head shots of the director of public relations, and for standing on a toilet seat and peaking over to the next stall to watch the only female chemist from the lab go to the bathroom. Much of this sounds like, and is, the "sexual frog down the back" kind of behavior.

Another kind of behavior involves employees at work who seem to be trying their hand at adult cable comedy. From my experience, even though there is a heightened sensitivity to sexual harassment in the workplace, the sexual jokes that are being verbally and electronically passed around today are more plentiful and more sexually explicit than ever. Many companies are aware of the sexual jokes traffic but don't know how to put a stop to it. And, ironically, these sound bites of sexual humor are often about sexual harassment, thanks to the focus on Washington.

The term *sexual harassment* covers a broad range of behaviors and an equally broad range of personality types. The person who tells filthy jokes to those he or she works with may never consider, for even a moment, pinning a coworker in the corner and asking for sex. The person who loves to hire only great-looking babes under the age of thirty might never even entertain the slightest thought of making a mild pass at any of them. And the fortyish executive who privately thinks women should stay at home and not be in his workplace in any significant position would hardly stand out as an offender of the current rules of gender bias. And, then, the woman who has had affairs with every boss she has worked for in the past ten years wouldn't be pointed out in the sexual harassment offenders lineup either. Psychologist and executive coach Sandor Blum believes identifying sexual harassers is difficult for untrained companies because there isn't a single profile of an offender. Blum has observed several different types of employees that fall under the category of harassers, although many of them don't share any common behavior patterns.

Those who can't seem to follow guidelines based upon equality, diversity, and fairness do, however, shoot out certain red flags to warn the rest of us. Blum spends a good deal of his practice time working with senior executives in need of one-on-one professional guidance in understanding what is expected from them as corporate leaders when it comes to sensitivity and diversity. He points out that many factors contribute to the way people behave in the workplace. Today's worker is yesterday's child, and some of the introductions employees have received regarding women, sexuality, ethics, even manners and social graces, would hardly meet the EEOC's standards of behavior.

A thought exercise I use during seminars is to ask employees to think about the first messages they received from family, friends, or community that told them how they should behave (within their gender) or how they should treat the opposite sex. Many men have offered and even defended their father's early words regarding what their father thought about women. Employees also recall (often unspoken) messages from their mothers. Those women who feared the powerful "head of the house," and the way they chose to react to the power figure, also factored in strongly in first impressions regarding "gender reaction," as I call it.

Often included in an explanation of sexual harassment is the phrase "in the eye of the beholder." Early educators of sexual harassment would stress that it isn't whether you think it's sexual harassment; it's whether the other person—the one it is happening to—thinks it is harassment. As one lawyer said, "If it feels like harassment, then it is harassment." Why is the range of tolerance so different from one person to another? Again, it goes back to background. I have worked with easily over 500 individuals who have experienced sexual harassment. The breaking point (the point at which they can't tolerate another person's behavior any more because of a sexually hostile working environment) may vary, but quite often it is triggered by both past experiences and present conditions.

When I finish taking a group of employees through thought exercises, we next address the invisible differences that people bring into the workplace. For example, if people were once victims of a serious crime, they will have a very low tolerance for any kind of threat happening to them again. People who are threatened by their bosses are going to feel very strongly about what is happening to them. People bring divorces, financial concerns, health problems, psychological challenges, and relationship woes, as well as their dreams and aspirations, right along with them when they go to work. These experiences, both the good and the bad, influence the way we do business and the way we treat others.

Research continues on the impact of sexual harassment on both its victims and the companies where it occurs. Understanding what someone who engages in sexual harassment might be thinking—and why this person needs or wants to behave in such a manner—can provide us with some very revealing clues about why this behavior continues to plague our workplaces. But before looking at inappropriate behavior at an individual level, we need to look at the culture we live and work in today and see what, if anything, is contributing to the kinds of people we are while at work.

TODAY'S WORKPLACE: LOCATED AT THE CORNER OF SOUTH PARK AND MELROSE PLACE

Many of the sitcoms on television depict the workplace as the *only* place to find love and sex, or at least to talk about it. In fact, psychologist Marion Gindes blames some of the confusion about the issue of sexual misconduct on these shows. According to Dr. Gindes, situation comedies often show the workplace as the characters' *total life*. Sitcom characters often have no friends or love interests outside their workplace. Anything sexual that will happen to them will happen at work. Coworkers talk openly about sexual desires, act out sexual antics, and send out the message that sex and the workplace are one and the same.

But television fictional characters and real working people do not live and work by the same laws. Distinguishing between the two appears to be a problem for some people. A 1994 study conducted by the

University of Dayton and led by communications professor Thomas Skill found numerous incidents of sexual harassment in prime-time sitcoms. In fact, the researchers found as many as nine per hour. Although some of the incidents did not take place in workplace settings, Skill felt that "they instill wrong ideas about sexual interaction which can be acted out at the office. . . ."

After reading about the study, I began a random survey of prime-time television, myself. I watched back-to-back sitcoms for three nights straight, looking for what I would consider acts of sexual harassment in the workplace. I stopped noting the inappropriate sexual incidents and started counting the clean scenes—it was less work. Ironically, there are three times the amount of sexual incidents on television today than Skill's study reported five years ago. What struck me was that sex, and all that goes with it, is more of a general story line than even the supposed plot of the night.

Characters talk openly about everything from orgasms, Viagra, condoms, phone sex, sleeping with their boss, breast sizes, penis sizes, sexual gratification, sex toys—you get the picture. One situation comedy even promoted its upcoming episode about a male worker fantasizing about watching two female workers have sex. And keep in mind that I only watched about seven half-hour shows. To the viewer who's sitting in front of the television, watching his or her favorite television characters break all the rules of sexual conduct in the workplace, it may just be a night of home entertainment. But the next day at work, it's back to real life, which does have its own set of rules. Unfortunately, many workers are not able to distinguish between the working world portrayed on television and the one they actually work in.

A DESCRIPTION IN GENERAL

Although there isn't a typical profile of a harasser, there are a few standout types of behavior that can allow us to draw some personality sketches of offenders.

THE SEXUAL OVERACHIEVER

This executive has spent his entire life focusing on winning. He's never lost anything. There have been no negative consequences, no losses in life so far. He has always measured his life in terms of wins, and he has racked up quite a few of them. Being powerful, and being perceived as being powerful, is extremely important to this person. It drives him. It makes him drive others. He often looks at women in terms of wins, and thinks of them as subjects of conquest. This guy found it relatively easy to get into the best schools, it was easy getting promoted, and it's always been easy when it comes to getting women. Getting a woman at work should be a slam-dunk. If for any reason she seems uninterested, it only means he should try harder, because, after all, the game is about winning. This executive doesn't hear or notice rejection because he is truly unfamiliar with the concept. With his power and position, quite frankly, he is certain that no one would ever turn him down.

THE PARTY ANIMAL

Thank you Monica and President Clinton and Marv Albert for all the material you've given the corporate stand-up comedian. It's about sex and it's "funny," so this person is going to be in on the sexual comedy network as far as he can. The party animal has partied to the maximum all though life. Anything on the edge, especially about sex, is a part of this person's talking points. Pushing the envelope, breaking all social and sexual rules, is what this individual wants to be known for. Generally loud, he is an organizer, and loves to shock people with his outspoken attitude on men and women, ethnic groups, politics, and, of course, sex. He may have come from a privileged family. He also may have been very competitive in some kinds of sports. He is actually sexually immature, with an infantile view of sexuality. According to Dr. Blum, this individual, unfortunately, may have learned his stuff from his father and may have had a mother who was the passive or subservient/adoring wife.

THE TRADITIONAL SEXIST

The traditional sexist is secretly still annoyed that women are in the workplace. He may adore the women in his immediate life (wife, sisters, daughters), but he places little value on the women he encounters in "his world." He has a low opinion of their purpose in his company, thinks a man could do a much better job than a woman who is holding a position, and totally disregards women's opinions when they are offered. Knowing that he must have "some women visible" at his company, he tries to place them in positions that have no real authority. He is very annoyed that women expect to work *and* have children and is the first to think of ways to get rid of a woman once she has had a child. At a seminar of CEOs, one president actually said to the group of twenty-five business leaders, "I cannot believe they expect to be a partner of our consulting firm and then want to have babies, too." He was looking for sympathy for being put in the horrible position of having to keep women that wanted families. It was 1997 when this particular CEO made this comment.

POWER MAIDENS

Much to the dismay of the feminists, many women in the workplace still believe they must use their sexuality while making a grand display of "deferring" to their more powerful male boss. Power maidens enjoy being around powerful men in the workplace. They will shop for them, feed them, listen to them, sacrifice their own personal lives for them, even appear to "worship" them, all the while allowing the power ranger to feel as though this is the kind of behavior all women in the department should exhibit. Most power maidens don't want to have a serious career of their own, but they like the excitement of being around someone who does. They thrive on the sexual energy surrounding their relationships with their powerful bosses and love being part of the "inner circle" surrounding their superior. Some may be unhappy with their own marriages or home lives, and find that this is a much better world for them to spend their time in.

THE FRONT MAN

Much like in primitive tribes, this male wants to impress the rest of the tribe of men. Because of feelings of insecurity and wanting to be accepted and liked by the other men, this man will make a point to harass or put women down sexually in front of male coworkers. Although these men realize they are being insulting, they feel like they are exhibiting acts of bravery, as ridiculous as that reasoning may be. In the case of primitive tribes, one hunter would run ahead of a group and attack the enemy. In this case, the front man strikes out at women.

BARE PARTS MANAGER

This individual is obsessed with body parts, sexual organs of both men and women, and keeps his or her focus on them. This is a result of immature sexual development. Instead of viewing someone as a whole person, the bare parts manager will look at a person in terms of "parts." Sarah with the nice ass; Beth with the great legs; did you notice the knockers on Carla? This individual comes from either gender. Women often reinforce this with comments like "Something in your pocket, or are you just glad to see me?" Monica and Linda talked "body parts" in their schoolgirlish discussions about the president's anatomy and those of other men Monica had "met."

According to Dr. Blum, men in this classification are accustomed to being surrounded by men. All their peers, all their friends, have been only men. They often drink hard, play hard, and have not rounded out their lives by having women as friends. In fact, they probably haven't even been in circles of both men and women with similar interests. These individuals are not interested in art or music, and generally only enjoy pastimes that preclude women, unless of course it's a chance to view some sort of pornography that focuses on women's body parts.

THE BOUNDARY HUNTER

This person constantly tests the most dangerous boundaries in life. This individual insufficiently sublimates his sex drive. Men who are boundary hunters are often considered to be sex addicts. Many people feel President Clinton is one. Dr. Blum points out that Clinton had no father to serve as a role model regarding sexual behavior, and this may be typical of other sexual addicts. There is no one in the person's life to tell him how to handle his sexual development. If a man is a sex addict, constantly risking marriages, jobs, reputation, everything, the search for affection is enormous and bigger than anything else in his life.

According to a May 10, 1999, *Fortune* magazine article on sexual addiction, a significant percentage of corporate America's workers have a serious problem satisfying their sexual appetites. Interestingly, the article also pointed out that workplace sex addicts are both men and women, and might very well be baby-boomers who came of age during the sexual revolution. "Put them into the anxiety-producing pressure cooker of today's work environment. Ratchet up the pressure to produce. Take away time to nurture real family relationships. Give access to cybersex, phone sex, prostitutes. Abracadabra: If a person is so inclined, he can fill his addictive need and 15 minutes later be back for a meeting."

THE THRILL-SEEKER

Also mentioned in the same *Fortune* article is what sexual disorder expert Patrick J. Carnes calls the thrill-seekers, and Carnes asserts that they are most commonly found on Wall Street. According to Carnes, "Wall Street is the worst. The sex down on Wall Street is unbelievable, with the prostitution and the porn." Carnes says that people who choose that kind of work tend to be thrill seekers to begin with. "Since it's Wall Street, there is no shortage of temptation."

Job stress combined with the daily thrill of "doing deals," can push a thrill-seeker who's already pumped up with adrenaline even further down the addiction road to thrills of a sexual nature. Despite the fact that today's workplace has been clearly and formally discouraged from offering access to sexual thrills, in some fast-lane work environments such as Wall Street, the availability to pick from entire menus of sexual thrills is as easy to order up as take-out food.

Although the thrill seeker may not have any interest in sexually harassing a coworker, his sexual addiction may spill over into his coworkers working environment creating a hostile work environment.

THE ISSUE OF FALSE CLAIMS— WHO IS MAKING THEM AND WHY?

False claims are not common, but they do occur. Usually they happen when the following conditions are present:

- An employee despises a superior for reasons that may or may not have to do with their direct working relationship. Issues that run the full range of jealousy (he has a beautiful house, he has a beautiful wife, he's successful, he's on a track, etc.) could be a motive for a false charge.

- A person is rejected or perceives he or she is rejected by a superior. This occurs when an employee has shown a romantic interest in a superior and has been directly or indirectly rejected.

- An employee has been made to feel inferior or lowly. This is a rare circumstance, but the employee may have been humiliated or treated poorly by the superior. This is a way to exert power over a superior.

- An employee hates the company he or she works for. Again, it is a rare occurrence, but an employee may feel he or she has been treated unfairly by the company even though sexual harassment did not occur.

- The employee hopes for financial gain. Like any lawsuit that is pursued for the sole purpose of money, the claim is made in the hopes that a company will settle it without determining whether or not it has merit.

···

CHAPTER 5

A Defining Moment

The working person's quick guidelines

to sexual harassment

I wish that I knew what I know now.

—Rod Stewart

GOOD SENSE AND SENSITIVITY

"To be perfectly honest, I never thought about what the definition of sexual harassment was, or is, until after it happened to
me. The moment it occurred, it was abundantly clear to me that
something terrible was happening, and I didn't know how to
get away from it. First, I was frightened; then I was frantic. I felt
powerless because I wasn't sure what *I* was supposed to do. I
don't know what was worse, the harassment or everything that
happened after. I guess I lost control when it happened to me,
and I never got it back. I wish I knew everything that I now
know. It all would have turned out so differently."

—Karen, age 32
Airline employee

HOW TO FIND TROUBLE AT WORK:
JUST GO LOOKING FOR IT

It seemed like a harmless stock picture of a cat walking down an alley
passing by five dogs. The caption underneath read, "It's Easy to Find
Trouble When You Go Looking for It." It hung on the wall, according
to an *Arizona Republic* article, for more than a year in a secluded area
of the Northern Arizona University (NAU) lock shop. The newspaper
reported, as did court records, that this is what occurred:

- The photo was placed on the shop wall by Ron Reline, a lock-
  smith, and Calvin Magness, a carpenter; and it was meant as a joke
  on their supervisor, Chuck Snelling. At the time, Snelling was at

odds with a number of women in the university's maintenance-stores department and front office. He felt the women weren't doing their jobs the way he thought they should. They were being sloppy with orders and payroll records. He complained to them, but he felt as though they didn't heed his advice.

- The women said that Snelling and his workers told "dumb blond" jokes and used vulgar language, and that Snelling seemed indifferent to an official warning that this created a hostile environment for them.

- Snelling said that he had ceased the inappropriate behavior and that his job was about safety for the students. One day Snelling's supervisor, John Woods, saw the photo and laughed.

- When the women learned of the photo, one went in and tore it down. She noted that the dogs were all named after the women who were at odds with Snelling, including herself. Mary Voves, who took the picture down, said that she felt "incredibly degraded" by the photo, and that it was her impression that they were female dogs—bitches—and that all these bitches were after Chuck the cat.

- Mary Voves met with the head of NAU's facilities management and asked that Snelling be removed. He called in Snelling and his boss, Woods, and explained to the men that it was a very serious situation, and that they could lose their jobs if it wasn't handled correctly.

- Reline and Magness, the two men who had put up the photo, were suspended but were offered a chance to apologize. One did and was reinstated. The other did not and was fired.

- Snelling was also fired, accused of sexual harassment and gender discrimination and of trying to discredit the maintenance-stores workers.

- Snelling's boss, Woods, was suspended for two days without pay because he had overall supervision of the area where the photo was posted.

- Woods lied that he had never seen the photo, but ultimately he went to management and told the truth, after committing perjury in legal proceedings. As part of Snelling's appeal to be reinstated to his position, he claimed that he thought the photo was "innocent," and his supervisor, who had seen the photo and laughed, apparently thought so, too.

- Charles Snelling was later rehired as lock-shop supervisor.

The moral of this story is *sexual harassment is not simple.* It is about the *need to think, and the need to know what you need to be thinking about and why.*

In fact, there are several good reasons to know what sexual harassment is:

- A bad experience with sexual harassment—whether you experience it or are accused of it—can change your life. This is not a dramatic statement. Watch the news or read the paper.

- Knowing how to handle sexual harassment—whether you have a claim or receive a complaint—can make the difference in preserving your job, your future, and the reputation of your company.

- There is a law that says it's illegal, and it's a law that is here to stay. Honest.

GET PERSONAL

Any of these reasons should be enough to make us want to take a moment and find out exactly what the legal definition of sexual harassment is, and to review some examples of behavior that may be viewed as inappropriate. Even if behavior falls into the "gray area," and it's unclear about whether it may or may not be sexual harassment under the strictest sense, it is still smart to stay away from such conduct. Most people think this kind of personal commitment will ruin their "engaging workplace personalities" and restrict them from being natural. It won't make you lose friends—as a matter of fact, it can only enhance your standing as an employee, whether you manage thousands of people or are just starting out in an entry-level position.

THE NEED TO KNOW

Sexual harassment in the workplace affects everyone. It has a profound effect on those who experience it, and often an equally adverse effect on those accused. No one within an organization escapes its impact. We need to know everything we can about sexual harassment and the misuse of power in the workplace. Our ability to manage this issue, as individuals and as companies, could quite possibly determine our success in our professional lives. It is as much about exercising good business practices as it is about being a responsible and sensitive employee. Today, being successful in the workplace requires us to make a commitment to do both.

Even if you have never experienced it, or never witnessed its adverse effects on individuals and companies that have, today's workplace requires that every employee understand the importance of maintaining a workplace free of any forms of discrimination and harassment. You need to make it your business to know all about this issue because your company, if it has not already done so, is about to make it company business to help you understand the seriousness of it in your workplace. You need to take it *personally,* because *it is all about your personal behavior.*

THE BASICS

After stating throughout several chapters that sexual harassment is tough to define, it's still important to come up with a basic definition of the kinds of behavior that are considered wrongful. To begin with, two important human aspects relate to the legal definition:

1. The act of sexual harassment causes harm. That is the basic reason why it is considered illegal. It hurts people. There has never been a claim or case of inappropriate behavior in the workplace that *hasn't hurt someone.* This is true even if the only people who will ever know it occurred are the one doing the harassing and the person or persons experiencing it.

2. Any retaliation against an individual who has complained about sexual harassment is as wrong as the harassment itself! Many employees and companies forget this important fact. *This action is just as illegal as sexual harassment.*

THE NEED TO THINK

It doesn't matter where we work or what kind of job we have—we all need to reach deep inside ourselves and consider three critical aspect of our thinking that can make all the difference in the way we live out our working lives:

- Our *attitude* toward other people in the workplace

- Our *ability* to use common sense in the choices and decisions we make that determine our behavior

- Our *approach* as we interact with others we work with and our desire to show respect for their uniqueness, their individuality, and, especially, their differences

THE NEED TO TAKE RESPONSIBILITY

Along with our job skills and professional backgrounds, we all bring into the workplace our own attitudes and approaches to life, work, people, and the way we feel about ourselves. These attitudes are often based partly upon where we grew up, how we were raised, and what kinds of outside influences have become part of our lives. We even carry with us to new jobs our feelings about the people we previously worked with and our attitudes toward them.

How we treat each other in the workplace is a personal choice and an important one. Respecting those we work with while understanding the significant advantages of being part of a working environment that promotes equality and fairness is the core of a good attitude. It is important to go beyond the legal definition of sexual harassment and simply think about how we can make a difference within our company, within our own work environment, by being responsible for our own behavior. If everyone took responsibility, the problem would barely exist.

THE LAW

In the United States, it is Title VII under the Civil Rights Act of 1964 that protects us from sexual harassment in the workplace. Title VII forbids an employer and those who work for the employer from committing certain kinds of employment discrimination. Most states and some cities have instituted similar laws to protect employees. Title VII protects employees from discrimination on account of their race, color, religion, sex, or national origin. It also prohibits retaliation against a person who files a charge of discrimination, participates in an investigation, or opposes an unlawful employment practice.

As mentioned in an earlier chapter, the federal agency responsible for enforcing Title VII is the Equal Employment Opportunity Commission (EEOC). Under the EEOC's definition of sexual harassment, it prohibits:

- Unwelcome sexual advances
- Requests for sexual favors
- Other verbal or physical conduct of a sexual nature

if:

- Submission to such conduct is made explicitly or implicitly a condition of employment.

- Submission to or rejection of such conduct is used as the basis for employment decisions.

- Such conduct has the purpose or effect of unreasonably interfering with an individual's work performance or creating an intimidating, hostile, or offensive work environment.

On November 19, 1991, the Civil Rights Act of 1991 was signed. Once the act became law, jury trials became available for complainants and compensatory damages (based upon intentional discrimination and unlawful employment practice) and punitive damages (based upon the size of the employer) could be awarded in successful suits.

On June 26, 1998, the Supreme Court issued two important decisions regarding sexual harassment. These decisions offered further clarification to the legal definition of sexual harassment by defining when an employer is liable for its supervisors' actions. In addition, the decisions made it clear that employers must take steps to have sound policies prohibiting sexual harassment, effective investigative procedures, and comprehensive training programs for all employees.

TYPES OF SEXUAL HARASSMENT RECOGNIZED BY LAW
QUID PRO QUO

Quid pro quo is defined as any action taken against an employee for refusing unwanted sexual advances by a superior. You can't ask or even hint to a subordinate or coworker that you would like him or her to have any type of sexual relationship with you in order for that person to get a raise, a job perk, a favorable review, a promotion, or better working conditions (fewer hours, more vacation days, fewer reports, etc.).

You cannot ask a person to have any type of sexual relationship with you to avoid losing his or her job. Even pressuring someone for dates or pushing to spend personal time together can be construed as sexual harassment. In fact, the courts have made it clear that you don't even need to *carry out* any threat of this nature to be guilty of sexual harassment. Just by saying what you might inflict puts another employee in a position where he or she feels that both job and personal well-being are being threatened. The threat is serious enough to cause significant damage.

HOSTILE WORK ENVIRONMENT

Hostile work environment is defined as unwelcome sexual conduct in a work environment which interferes with an employee's work performance or creates an intimidating, hostile, or offensive environment. The following examples, depending on the total circumstances, may constitute sexual harassment:

Making comments about looks

Using language of a sexual nature

Telling sexual jokes and stories

Sharing details of sexual life

Revealing sexual fantasies

Giving unwanted sexual compliments and making innuendoes

Engaging in unwanted physical touching

Twisting business topics into sexual topics

Staring

Displaying sexually suggestive materials in the workplace

Those employees who help create a workplace environment that is unsuitable for other people to work in because these individuals are continually exposing and subjecting others to sexual remarks, sexual jokes, or any behavior of a sexual nature are polluters of the workplace atmosphere and guilty of creating a hostile work environment. Employees should not bother others at work by continuously saying or doing things of a sexual nature so that they annoy, upset, or offend others to the point of interfering with their job or their ability to do their job. People can't work effectively if they feel as though an unwanted "sexual climate" exists around them. They certainly can't be productive if they happen to be the direct targets of such abusive behavior.

Even if you are discussing something of a sexual nature with just one other coworker (who might even be your closest friend) and others in the workplace overhear you, you may be contributing to or even creating a sexually hostile work environment. The workplace is not our home. It belongs to everyone.

EXAMPLES OF INAPPROPRIATE BEHAVIOR

Because these two types of sexual harassment, hostile work environment and quid pro quo, are identified as the general categories of improper conduct in the workplace, it is important to understand what some of the specific types of behavior are—and why they should not take place where you work.

INAPPROPRIATE REMARKS
AND SHADES OF IMPLICATIONS

Don't refer to a coworker or a subordinate as a sexual being or refer to his or her physical looks in a sexual manner. Saying she's "a ten" after a job interview or making a remark that you would like to work on Sean's team because he is so hot-looking says nothing for fairness and equality in the workplace. The workplace is not a bar.

SEXUAL GENERALIZATIONS
AND SEXUAL PUT-DOWNS

Don't insinuate that others at work are of lesser quality, have less ability, or are gender-challenged because of their sex. You've heard the hurtful remarks both men and women have made about each other over the years. "Just like a man, always thinking of sex," or "You know how women are. Kristen is no different." Making sexual generalizations or sexual put-down remarks lets your coworkers know that you have an unfair attitude toward the other sex. It lessens their chances of being treated fairly and being respected for their contributions and performances, regardless of their gender. Think about what you are saying and what it may mean to others. Generalizations are usually taken very personally by those who hear them.

TERMS OF ENDEARMENT

The way you address your coworker sends powerful messages about your attitude toward him or her. Calling a coworker or subordinate inappropriate names such as "cutie," "blondie," "honey," "dear," or "sweetie" should be completely avoided in the working environment. Even if there is no sexual message behind these terms, they send a message to other employees that either you don't value them as a part of the team or you are thinking of them in terms of their gender, age, physical looks, or sexual identity. They don't feel valued or respected and often feel their roles are irrelevant and their contributions unnoticed, even though that may or may not have been your intention when you used such an "endearing term."

A COWORKER BY ANY OTHER NAME IS JUST NOT THE SAME

Taking how you address your coworkers a step further, be aware that no nicknames for a coworker or subordinates that you, or anyone else (except the coworker), happen to think of are appropriate at work. Nicknames are acceptable *only* when an employee asks that you call him or her by a nickname. It is also important that the name is not sexual and is appropriate for the work environment.

DANGER ZONES AND OUT-OF-BOUND COMPLIMENTS

Part of building quality working relationships in the workplace is showing others that you not only value their work, but think highly of them as individuals. Sincere compliments directed to those you work with help to build important relationships and provide necessary feedback to your coworkers.

On the other hand, "compliments" of a sexual nature are destructive, dangerous, and often illegal. "Sarah, I wish you would wear more short skirts, just like the one you have on, because I think you have great legs and I enjoy coming to work and looking at them" is probably not a compliment that Sarah wants to hear from her boss or her coworker. It will likely make her think that her boss or coworker is thinking of her in a sexual way, and that could upset her and make her feel uncomfortable.

In one case, a worker was shocked when a coworker took offense at his remark about how he liked the way her dress fit. He insisted he was just delivering a harmless compliment. For the woman he directed his "compliment" to, it was anything but. She took what he said as a sexual remark because he was commenting on her body. To her, the remark sounded sexual. And it was unwanted. She especially didn't like the way he delivered it. "Oh, ye—a-a-h, Sar—a-a-h. Some dress. I'm saying that I'm lovin' the way it fits that body of yours!" Anything of a sexual nature said to another at work is out-of-bounds, even if you think if it complimentary. Keep in mind that you always need to be sensitive to what another person's own definition is of an unwanted sexual advance. An unwanted, unwelcome sexual remark can often be enough to cross the line into a danger zone of a coworker.

PERSONAL SPACE INVASION

In defining personal space, although the lines are certainly invisible, the need for our own space is very clear. A very subtle type of unwanted behavior often involves individuals who "invade" someone else's personal space while on the job.

A common example is something most of you have seen or experienced or maybe even recall doing yourself at one time. There are those who think of themselves as "the body/dress adjusters," implementing their own grooming/fashion code for others in the workplace. Usually uninvited, they will take it upon themselves to pull a thread on your skirt or jacket, pick lint off your suit, adjust or change your hair style, reposition your hair ornament, snap a man's suspenders to change their location, touch and pull on a man's tie, play with earrings and jewelry, smooth a shoulder pad down, straighten a hemline, undo a button, or even reach into someone's pocket. They often think they are helpful and usually are not motivated sexually. But sometimes someone is being exactly that. Rather than be misunderstood, it is much better to refrain from touching coworkers when they haven't asked for your help, even if it seems needed at the time. Personal space is important to everyone, especially in the workplace.

RUBBING OTHERS THE WRONG WAY

Continuing with the importance of respecting others, refraining from unwanted physical contact is essential in creating a workplace free of sexual harassment. Simply put, here's some of what does *not* belong in the workplace:

Back and neck rubbing (especially walking up to someone who is busy at his or her computer)

Kissing

Knee touching

Rubbing up against someone's leg under a conference table or desk

Leaning over on someone in the company elevator

Hand-holding

Bumping and brushing up against another person

Prolonged intense staring

Unwanted physical touching in the workplace is one of the most common elements found in claims of harassment.

PORNOGRAPHIC OR SUGGESTIVE LITERATURE AND LANGUAGE

According to an Associated Press article, writer John Flesher points out the importance of understanding that although the First Amendment prevents the government from stifling speech, private employers are under no such constraints, as a teacher in Traverse City, Michigan, learned,

> Hired to teach computer technology at a marketing company, Cameron Barrett suggested his trainees might learn something by checking out his Web page, where he published his own fiction. Some women staff members did, and were shocked by the violent and sexually explicit passages. They complained to their boss, and Barrett was fired.

Pornographic and sexual literature pinned up on bulletins boards, taped over someone's desk, hung in work areas, or sent to coworkers via interoffice mail, e-mail, fax, or voice mail while at work are all unacceptable in today's workplace. So are sexual chats over the Internet and pornographic and sexual artwork and computer screen-savers. Even if a sexual cartoon, picture, or joke didn't originate with you, if you are responsible for forwarding it, passing it along, or helping to distribute it in any way, you are just as responsible as the person who first brought it into your workplace. Your company provides you with the use of computers, faxes, telephones, copy machines, etc., to help you do your job. Improper use of company property for other purposes may contribute to a hostile work environment for your coworkers.

SEXUAL JOKES

Many employees mistakenly believe that telling or making sexual jokes in the workplace is part of daily life, something we can all look forward to, and a suitable way to relieve stress and job pressure. The flow of sexual jokes in today's workplace is almost epidemic and one of the most prevalent behavior patterns in hostile work environment situations.

Sexual jokes that are made during meetings or staff functions, or even told over one cubicle wall to the next, do not belong in the workplace. The jokes are almost always at the expense of someone, and tell workers loud and clear that a coworker doesn't care whom he or she might be offending.

SEXUAL ANTICS

These so-called clever antics supposedly are done in the name of fun. Not only do they occur at the expense of the person the joke is being played on, but they usually offend most of those who happen to see or hear of it. For example, hiring a stripper to come to your office to entertain one of your coworkers on his or her birthday, engagement, or retirement is tasteless and an out-of-place act that does not belong in the workplace—or any place where employees are gathered in an official capacity. Other common inappropriate sexual antics are sexual gag gifts given to coworkers, including cakes decorated with a sexual motif.

THE SILENT WORD ON SEXUAL HARASSMENT

Many people have problems with the words *unwanted* and *unwelcome* in the definition of sexual harassment. When people perceive someone else's actions as unwanted, there is a good chance that they won't *tell you* that. In fact, they may laugh at your joke, smile when you touch his or her knee, even go along with the sexual prank you are planning all the while wishing you would be run over by a bus before the next business day. How do you know it is unwanted? You can't rely on the signals the other person may be giving to you.

But why would a person go along with something if it was unwanted? There are a number of reasons why someone won't let you know that something sexually based is unwanted:

The Number One Reason for Silence: Fear of Power.
You may be the president of the company. Everyone who works for the company ultimately works for you, and thus is afraid to tell you the truth. A few years ago, a company president wanted a piece of sculpture that he had purchased in Europe to be prominently displayed in the company's intercorporate offices. The sculpture had two nude figures intertwined. It was a work of art, the president said. Several employees who had to walk by it numerous times a day said that it embarrassed them because the figures were, in their words, "doing it." The president then asked all the employees if they minded the sculpture. They said, "Oh no. No problem at all." Obviously, at least some were afraid to give an honest answer.

Other Common Reasons Why People Won't Speak Up.
Frequently, people won't speak up against sexual harassment because they are afraid they will make you angry and then you will retaliate. You might cut them out of good projects, make them work unreasonable hours, start giving them poor reviews, no longer consider them a valuable employee—or, worse, fire them.

Specifically, if people lose their job:

- They will lose their paycheck.
- They may not be able to pay their rent or mortgage.
- They will lose their pension.
- It will look suspicious on their résumé if they walk or get fired from this job.

- They will no longer have the security that goes along with having a job.

- They are afraid of the kind of recommendation they will get. If someone complains of sexual harassment, would you still give him or her a good recommendation?

- Their reputation will likely suffer.

- They may not be able to send their children to college or help their elderly parents.

- They will lose their medical benefits. This is especially distressful if a spouse has medical problems.

- They don't want the publicity or public exposure that sometimes comes with lodging charges of sexual harassment.

Some people put up with sexual harassment because other than the horrible behavior, they like what they do and where they work. Others have a dream, and part of making that dream come true means sticking it out for a while longer even if it means putting up with a jerk.

CORPORATE ROMANCES
TIME-HONORED AND BOUND TO HAPPEN

Despite concerns about sexual harassment, corporate romances are inevitable. People meet on the job, and sometimes they like each other. They date, and sometimes they marry. This is not new, and it's not a bad thing. And based upon the amount of time people spend working, it is not surprising that the workplace is a likely meeting place for potential spouses.

THE COMPANY SOCIAL CALENDAR— PROMOTING TOGETHERNESS

People meet on the job in a number of ways. Many companies strive to make employees feel they are part of the "company team" by sponsoring and endorsing company functions. These include a wide range of extracurricular activities—company outings, mixers, performance and achievement clubs held in tropical resorts or ski resorts, softball teams, and executive retreats for high-level management. People who meet this way sometimes develop long-term relationships. On the other hand, sometimes these meetings result in short-term sexual mayhem.

Many of the claims I am brought into companies to address entail one or more incidents that occurred at a conference or out-of-town event. I have had to investigate a range of indiscriminate activities that have included everything from male managers running naked in front of female coworkers, people surfing and skiing in the buff, coworkers having intercourse in front of other coworkers, poker games that have spun out of control, strippers going beyond dangerous entertainment, drunken brawls where workers can't recall who did what, and instances of attempted rape and physical abuse. The partying and the revelry get quickly out of hand, and many employees find themselves involved in one-time affairs with coworkers that they would never consider back on home turf.

In addition, the annual holiday parties are still a problem, even with the heightened awareness that wearing a lamp shade on your head and kissing your secretary's neck to celebrate Christmas are no longer acceptable yuletide celebrations.

Some companies recognize that properly organized company func-tions that fall mainly under the heading of social gatherings are still good for promoting the spirited mission statement of an organization. It does seem true that if people who work together like each other and get along socially, they will ultimately work better together.

And further still, companies are also realizing that they need to address employees as more than workers. They need to acknowledge the "total lives" of other employees and help them strike a balance between their professional and personal lives. Stress is a major health problem facing working people. Companies believe they can help reduce this stress by providing company channels to encourage employees to find ways of enjoying themselves. Providing social opportunities within the framework of the company is one way employers can offer outlets for overworked employees.

WHO GETS INVOLVED?

No matter what the circumstances, some people simply won't get involved with anyone at work. Others are a little more relaxed about establishing such a straight personal policy but are very careful about whom they get involved with on the job. Then there are others who view their jobs as opportunities for brief affairs, long-term involvements, or the end of the search for a possible mate. Each position involves making personal decisions based upon your priorities.

IT JUST HAPPENS

Most men and women who begin dating a coworker know that it didn't require a company party to get things started. Initiating a consensual sexual relationship with someone at work is something that employees say "just sort of happened." But along with this natural thing between two sexual beings, workers face serious dilemmas, and need to address them promptly and thoughtfully. It is critical that individuals know that they need to be aware of corporate vs. personal boundaries when they socialize so dangerously close to the edge of the sexual harassment cliff. The two people involved need to establish, understand, and follow certain rules. Their priorities need to be very clear, and that is usually where most of the problems arise.

DANGEROUS LIAISONS:
SUPERIOR-SUBORDINATE RELATIONSHIPS

Certain relationships between people who work together can and do immediately jeopardize jobs and long-term careers as well as endanger the environment of the workplace. When a person dates or becomes sexually involved with the person he or she reports to, both parties are asking for trouble. The two people involved might be tremendous assets to an organization, but the mere existence of their relationship automatically puts a strain on the workplace environment and risks both their careers.

The Involved Supervisor.   This person is jeopardizing his or her working relationship with other subordinates, a future with the company, and the ability to manage people objectively. The supervisor, as an agent of the company, is always acting on behalf of the company regarding any involvement with an employee.

The Involved Subordinate.   The involved subordinate may not get a fair break. In an effort to appear fair to other employees and to avoid being accused of showing preferential treatment, a superior might give less positive employment reviews to the involved subordinate than the subordinate deserves. If, on the other hand, the involved subordinate receives positive reviews during the affair, it is likely that others will question whether the subordinate earned high marks on the basis of ability. Other employees also might view the involved subordinate as "an informant among the ranks" for the boss, and thus the subordinate probably will experience a degree of isolation as a member of a department team.

The Coworkers, the Department, the Company.   When a superior is involved with one subordinate, others in the department are likely to feel a range of negative emotions and concerns. Resentment of the affair is a common reaction. This attitude can affect a whole department or even an entire company. If the affair ends, charges of sexual harassment may be brought by one of the previously involved parties, which automatically brings the company into the picture.

Considering the Options. The options in a superior-subordinate relationship aren't that hard to figure out, although many people, when caught between their job and an affair, have a tough time facing them. Here are some of the ways people manage (or don't manage) their affairs:

> **Keep the relationship underground.** Don't let anyone know that you are seeing each other. However, keep in mind that even if you spend a lot of time and energy concealing your affair, others may eventually find out anyway.
>
> **Leave the company.** Is the relationship important enough to both of you to consider making changes in either or both of your careers? This is where priorities need to be very clear.
>
> **Tell the company.** It is better for two people to be proactive about their relationship and mention it to their company so that the company can help the couple determine what professional arrangement is best for everyone. Companies do like to help responsible couples find a good solution—and the solution could enable both employees to stay with the company.

DATING COWORKERS

Coworkers are those who don't report to you, or whom you don't report to, and ideally don't work in your department or division. Dating a coworker is not considered sexual misconduct as long as the relationship takes the following into consideration:

> **Don't abuse the privileges of the workplace by misusing time and expense money to pursue a personal relationship.** The following is a tale of blatant abuse. A company found out that two employees were misusing company time to engage in what was an extramarital affair for both. The company wanted to get rid of

them because of the affair but ended up firing them for misusing company funds for unauthorized "overnight outings." For the company it was an easier way to dismiss the employees without having to directly address their affair.

Be aware of your company's policy. Some companies have policies prohibiting dating.

Try to keep your relationship with a coworker private. You are only hurting yourself by discussing it with other coworkers. The person you are dating should behave in the same manner and should respect your need for privacy and confidentiality. Don't e-mail personal sentiments, don't defend your lover in meetings, and make no public displays of affection in the workplace. One woman walked in on her boss, who was lying across his drawing board with another employee. She said she felt like she had walked into their bedroom. It was two in the afternoon, and she needed to get copy over to a newspaper in time for a deadline. Her boss was very angry with her for walking in on him. She felt that his anger was unjustified. It was.

Follow the proper ways of approaching someone that you are interested in seeing socially. Be very clear and upfront about your desire to see someone on a social rather than professional level. If you ask a coworker out once and he or she declines, you should never ask the person out again. One man told me that as a single man at a very large company, he had a policy that worked for him. If he asked a coworker out and she declined, he told her to let him know if she ever changed her mind. That way, he could never be accused of pressuring someone for dates.

THE DEFINITION OF SEXUAL HARASSMENT FOR EVERYDAY PEOPLE IN THE EVERYDAY WORLD

Sexual harassment occurs within a workplace (and the workplace can be any setting in which people may find themselves in connection with their job) when a working person subjects another working person to sexual behavior that is unwelcome, is unwanted, and is considered offensive by those experiencing it. This behavior can occur and be repeated in a number of forms. It can be something said, something acted out, something written, electronically or otherwise, or just the presence of "something" that is considered sexually demeaning to either gender.

Employees have an obligation to report sexual harassment, and companies have an obligation to conduct a prompt investigation of the allegation in a fair and expeditious manner. It is against the law to retaliate against an individual who has complained about sexual harassment.

Getting Inside

The Hidden Costs of Internal Affairs

CHAPTER 6

Anatomy of a Sexual Harassment Case

A reputation may be repaired, but people always keep their eyes on the place where the crack was.

The harassment principle. Every act of sexual misconduct which is not addressed immediately and appropriately will have a profound and unmanageable impact far beyond the damages of the original offensive behavior. The wildfire, the second-order effects, spreads to the core of an organization and can greatly damage relationships and reputations for an indefinite, immeasurable, and costly period of time.

Those companies that have experienced a sexual harassment or sexual misconduct case gone sour know that they will never again underestimate the effects of such a case. There are several hidden impacts that most companies don't think of when they mentally dismiss a person with a claim or overlook the claim itself. Most companies think that cases gone awry are about money. That is only partly true. What is also lost are time and trust. And in regard to time, it is always the time lost by people whose time is most expensive and perceived as most valuable to the company.

In quid pro quo cases of sexual harassment, it is usually a manager who is being accused. His or her duties as manager are often affected while the claim is being addressed. From the time the claim is reported until the time it is resolved, that manager will be key in helping the company respond. If the company fails to resolve the complaint internally, the claim could take as long as eight years in a federal court system. Although certainly not a daily task, the manager has to be available at very short notice to assist the company in defending itself.

BACKGROUND OF THIS CASE STUDY

This chapter describes what happens when a claim of sexual harassment moves through a company. Our fictional company has a sexual harassment policy on record but has never done any training. The human resources department consists of three people, although one person in the department just takes care of benefits for employees. The company started out as a four-person operation and grew quickly, always focusing on expanding its client billings—and like most growth operations, lagging in addressing internal issues.

RIPE FOR A CLAIM, READY FOR A CASE

Williams Casey Inc. is a midwestern advertising agency specializing in food and consumer products. The agency is co-owned by two men, Dave Williams and Richard Casey. David Williams is the creative director, and Rich Casey handles all the administrative and business aspects of the organization. Rich Casey is responsible for new business, while Dave handles the creative product of the agency. Twenty, sometimes twenty-five, people work in the creative division of the main office in Chicago. Ten other people work in the smaller offices of the agency, one in New York and one in Washington. In total, the agency employs almost 185 people.

The agency has annual billings of $18 million. Almost $8 million of the total billing comes from a client based in Chicago. That client was a founding client that was brought in largely due to Dave Williams's relationship with the president of Lake Farm Frozen Foods, Nathan Henderson, beginning almost ten years ago. Dave Williams has a strong allegiance to Nat Henderson, and feels as though he owes Nat for the start of his business. On the other hand, the account was only worth about $1.2 million when the company started out. It was Dave who was largely responsible for cultivating the continued relationship with Lake Farm Foods.

Michelle Robertson is one of the art directors (loose term for senior members of the account teams from the creative department). Michelle is the daughter of a friend of Nat's but didn't go through him to get her job. She applied after finishing at Pratt, an art school, and got the job on her own merit, only casually mentioning that she knew Nathan Henderson growing up. Michelle has worked at the agency for eight years. She works under Dave Williams's supervision.

Recently, Dave hired Steve Telleck as a day-to-day creative director for the Chicago office. Steve had a good mix of creative and management skills. Dave wanted to be freed up to be able to work on new business pitches with his partner. The agency was growing so rapidly he needed to make room for himself to best serve the agency. At this point, the agency was going after a major food store chain, Golden Grocer Foods. Landing this account would push the agency into a much larger category and require that it open offices in Atlanta and Minneapolis. Six months earlier, when he had hired Steve, Dave told the entire staff about the change. If the agency obtained the new business, Steve would be the point person on that piece of business; and Dave told Michelle that she would be running the Lake Farm Foods account. Michelle had always wanted to have creative control over the account. She loved the people there and felt as though she knew what they needed. Meanwhile, Steve was learning the agency in his new position, and would be ready to take over the Golden Grocer campaign once the account was secured.

Steve's management style was very different from Dave's. Dave rolled his sleeves up and looked at creating advertising campaigns from the drawing board, with staff grouped around throwing out ideas. Once an idea was voiced, anyone could take the idea and run with it—there were no restrictions in the initial creative process. Steve worked differently. He had come from a big ad shop and had a much more controlled approach to the business. Meetings were much more formal, and they were held in the conference room. The members of the creative team presented their ideas one by one, and they were gradually eliminated. If Steve was interested in an idea, he worked individually with the person, especially during the concept development aspect of the creative process.

For several months, Michelle was dismayed because all her ideas for various campaigns were passed up. Finally, after Steve had been with the agency for over four months, he liked an idea Michelle presented for Lake Farm Foods. Her television and radio commercial ideas were great, he said, but he would need to work with her more on the storyboards of the campaign. It was a huge promotion for the client with a substantial budget attached to it. Michelle and Steve immediately began putting in long hours to get the campaign ready for the client to see. Steve and Michelle worked hard and got along well. Michelle still preferred the old days and the old ways of working with Dave, but she was happy that Steve was appreciating her work.

The day of the presentation, Steve and Michelle went to the client's corporate headquarters. The campaign was accepted, and the client was so thrilled with the work that the media budget was increased. The meeting ended after six, and in the car on the way back to the office, Steve suggested a celebration over dinner. Michelle agreed and even picked out the restaurant. At dinner, Steve started to get into personal issues with Michelle. She liked Steve, neither of them was married, and she didn't feel uncomfortable talking to him about her life. He started to get affectionate, but it wasn't anything Michelle felt that she couldn't handle. Steve dropped Michelle off at her car back at the office, and drove away. He didn't push anything more.

The next day at the staff meeting, Steve praised Michelle to the others, and said it was the best creative work he had seen in a long time. Michelle was bothered that he went on too much about it. She wasn't sure whether Steve was saying those things because her work was that good or because he had a really good time with her the night before. A few days later Steve asked her to lunch. He was very friendly during lunch and continued to rave about her work and actually about her. He mentioned that they needed to get together for a few hours that afternoon to work out a few details. They ended up meeting for several hours.

That night, Steve called Michelle at home to mention a couple of things he said that he forgot to mention during the day. In the conversation, he gradually started to talk about more personal things, mentioning that he thought she must have someone in her life, as pretty as she was. In fact, he was surprised to catch her at home. That was the first night of many that Steve began calling her at home. In the two weeks that followed, Steve even stopped over one night (Michelle didn't even know he knew where she lived) to bring over some ad copy that he thought she should look at. He explained that it just came in when he was leaving and he thought she would like to see it before the next day.

It was when she was sitting on her couch with Steve, looking at the ads, that Steve made his move. Within minutes he was all over her. She resisted and stood up when she could. She told him that she was on her way out to meet a couple of friends and that she needed to go. She never acknowledged his attempt, thinking it was best to let it go. After Steve left, Michelle went over to her friend's apartment. When she returned, she found three hang-ups on her answering machine. The fourth message was from Steve, saying he hoped he hadn't upset her.

The next day, she treated him as she always did, and he seemed unfazed, too. He asked if she could grab lunch with him and go over a couple of things. She went to lunch, and he began the lunch by talking about her being promoted to be the permanent account manager for Lake Farm Frozen Foods. She was the only one qualified, and the client thought highly of her. With that, he started to come on to her, leaning over to kiss her ear and push his hand up her leg past her skirt hemline. She grabbed his hand and pushed it back. She let him know that she had no interest in a personal relationship with him. None at all. It couldn't be like that. She had a policy about dating anyone she worked with— let alone for—and she hoped he understood that. He took his hand off her thigh, and seemed to understand. She was extremely relieved.

However, that night, Steve called her at home to talk more about "their relationship." She pointed out that there was no relationship. The next day, Steve seemed more agitated. He told Michelle to grab her coat and material on Lake Farm. They needed to meet with the client. She left with Steve and found out in the car that there was no meeting. He just wanted to talk to her about his feelings for her. Michelle was deeply concerned—her straightforward approach of dealing with Steve wasn't working, and she didn't know what to do next. She asked Steve to take her back to the office. Not yet, he said, as he pulled the car into a city park near the lakefront. As he stopped the car, he tried to pull her to him. Michelle became very upset and pushed him away, begging him to take her back to the office. Michelle finally jumped out of the car and walked to a busy main street and hailed a cab. She headed back to work and went straight to her office. Steve was becoming a nightmare, and she didn't know how responsible she was.

Michelle told the receptionist she was sick and left for the day. Her telephone rang repeatedly that evening, but she didn't answer it. The next day at work, she knew she had to see Steve about certain deadlines but couldn't bring herself to go into his office. When she knew he was in a meeting in the conference room, she hurried into his office and dropped the papers that needed signatures on his desk. At the end of the day, he brought them back to her. He was very quiet and offered no explanation for his behavior the day before.

On the following day, there was a staff meeting. Steve made the usual weekly department announcements but included two more. One was that the agency had officially won the Golden Grocer Foods account. The other was that he was going to make a few changes with assignments. Michael Roth would be heading the account team for Lake Farm once Steve moved to Golden Grocer. Steve mentioned that he had given this change a lot of thought and that Dave had looked to him for guidance in selecting the right person to take over the account. The department applauded Michael.

Michelle felt her face burning. She was the right person. Dave had all but promised her that she would be promoted to that position. What could Steve have said to make this happen? Again, Michelle left for the day, unable to look at Steve or anyone else. The next day, she ran into Dave in the hall, as he was returning from a trip to the corporate head-quarters of Golden Grocer after officially signing the company as a client. Before she could ask, Dave told her he knew of Steve's decision to promote Michael. He really had thought Steve would just naturally pick her to run the account, but he had given over the decision to Steve and couldn't interfere at this late point. He said he was surprised that she wasn't selected, but when he spoke with Steve the night before, Steve had given a lot of valid points about Michael's work, particularly his management skills. Steve didn't think Michelle was "ready" to manage such an important account. Dave was sorry, very sorry, but his hands were tied. He thinks the world of her, of course, always has, always will. He left her standing in the hall.

Steve officially became in charge of the creative product for the entire agency. Dave was vice chair and spent most of his time in the Atlanta office so he could be near Golden Grocer headquarters. Michelle's job wasn't really director status anymore, she noticed. Maybe it never had been. Dave had always been so loose about titles. They never mattered that much to her then. She did some work on both of the major accounts and did a lot of work on the smaller accounts that the agency maintained. She reported to Steve officially, but he never had anything to do with her really. Michael treated her like a lowly employee, and everytime Dave was in the Chicago office, he seemed uncomfortable when he ran into Michelle. Only three weeks had passed since the day Steve had grabbed her at the lake, but it seemed like three years to Michelle.

THE PATH OF A PLAINTIFF

Michelle was certain that she had experienced sexual harassment. She knew that the handbook the agency had been working on had been in revision stages for about three years. It was ridiculous, the personnel manager had said once at a general meeting, that the company was an ad agency and yet it couldn't get a simple internal publication completed and distributed. Michelle checked the file in the art department to see if there was a copy file for the new handbook. There was—

and a sexual harassment policy was in it. It said that you could report the harassment to either one of the partners or the personnel director or your supervisor. She decided to go to Dave Williams even though he had been dodging her since Steve announced Michael's promotion. She called his secretary and found out that Dave would be in the Chicago office on Friday. She set up an appointment for the first thing Friday morning. That way she wouldn't have time to lose her nerve, and she still had a few days to think about what she was going to say.

On Thursday, in one rare moment when Steve actually spoke directly to her after the staff viewed a commercial reel that just came from the production house, he told her he knew that she was meeting with Dave on Friday. He wondered why she asked for a meeting with him. Dave was out of the loop on the day-to-day goings-on in their office. If she had any questions about anything, she should come to him or Michael. She lied to Steve and said she was talking to Dave about some pro bono work one of her professional trade association groups wanted the agency to do—and the group had asked that she talk to Dave because of his friendships with some of the members. She knew that Steve didn't believe her, but she left the room before he had a chance to say anything else.

The next day, Dave was polite to Michelle but seemed guarded. She thought that Steve had probably talked to Dave about his displeasure in Michelle going above Steve's head. She told Dave that Steve had sexually harassed her. He had physically assaulted her in his car and had called her repeatedly at home. And when she told him clearly that she had no intention of getting involved with him, he pulled her opportunity to work with Lake Farm Foods away from her.

Dave was silent for several minutes and carefully spoke. He told Michelle that Steve had "come clean." He had gone to Dave and told him that Michelle and Steve had been "involved," but he had ended it when he realized it wasn't the right thing to be doing as her boss. He also told Dave that Michelle wasn't taking the breakup well and seemed to be terribly preoccupied at work about all of it. Steve felt awful that

Michelle was taking it so hard, but he just couldn't be involved with her. It wasn't professional. He needed to manage her, and so he needed to keep her at arm's length. He was afraid that Michelle might try to report something like this after she didn't get the promotion that she hoped for, but he still had to promote the best person.

Michelle was shocked and denied that she was ever involved. Dave was nervous about her reaction, and seemed really unhappy that she was so upset. She begged Dave to believe her. There was no affair, she told him—it was just Steve who had made the advances. Dave kept shifting around in his chair and said that if she was his daughter, he would tell her she needed to learn something from all this. It is not good to get a crush on a supervisor, even though Steve is young, single, and available. He told her that Steve had a girlfriend, a nice woman, and that Steve and his girlfriend and Dave and his wife had met for dinner last weekend. Steve had expressed concern that Michelle's obsession with him would be a problem with his girlfriend. He hoped that it wouldn't.

Michelle couldn't speak. Dave suggested she talk to personnel and see about tapping into the employee assistance program available for psychological counseling. She left Dave's office and, once again, left for the day. She had been at the Williams Casey agency since she graduated. She had been an award-winning artist, bringing awards into the agency for her work. The agency had benefited from that. She had worked hard on the key accounts of the agency. She had had a great relationship with the founding partners of the agency. She came from a good Chicago family, connected to the community. How could Steve, someone new to the agency, spin such a twisted tale so fast to ruin her job?

Michelle was furious. She called her father and mother and told them what was happening. Her father told her to call his old roommate at the University of Chicago. He was a partner at the Chicago office of Mason, Cadbury and Weiss, a big law firm that had a good employment labor law practice. Michelle made an appointment with attorney John Weiss for the next day. She left a voice mail for the receptionist at

Williams Casey, saying that she had a dentist appointment the next morning and would be a little late. John Weiss had told her to write down everything that had happened and to have dates of everything that occurred. The next day she met with Weiss, and he took the case. He said that he thought there was no point in dealing with anyone at the agency except the two partners. He told her that he would have letters hand-delivered to both partners letting them know that Michelle had retained legal counsel to help her resolve the employment matter facing her. In the letter he stated that if they didn't take her claim and concern seriously and act promptly, Michelle would file a claim with the EEOC and pursue legal action.

BUILDING A DEFENSE

When Rich Casey got the letter from Michelle's attorney, he couldn't believe what he was reading. He had no idea that there were any problems with the Chicago creative department. In fact, Dave Williams had been calling Steve Telleck his golden boy. His partner thought Telleck was terrific. Michelle had worked for the agency for almost eight years. She had always been a great employee—she was so talented. Dave had mentored her through the creative department for eight years. He had to know something about this.

When Rich Casey and Dave Williams got together to discuss the letter from the lawyer, Casey was furious. How could you know about this problem and not let me know! This could be a real disaster. Michelle's parents are good friends with the Hendersons, aren't they? The partners made a conference call to their attorneys to ask how they should respond to the letter. The company's attorneys told the partners not to overreact. They said they needed to meet with Steve to hear his side of the story. They also asked if the agency had a sexual harassment policy, had they done any training, and if Steve was hitting on anyone else. As they talked, they decided they should get together in person. The lawyers also requested a separate meeting with personnel. It was decided that the partners would drop everything for the next day and meet with the attorneys so that they could draft a response.

The call was still not over. The questions continued. Had the company offered to do an investigation of the charge Michelle made? Did Dave tell her that the company took charges of sexual harassment seriously? OK, they would deal with this—but they needed to have more information on the employee who was doing the charging and the one being charged. Could the partners put together some sort of background profile on both employees? Include their employment history, any other problems, etc. Her attorney, John Weiss, is very good at these cases. He wouldn't take it if he didn't have some idea that she could win. Did the agency have any women managers? No? Well, they would have to deal with that. That could be a problem—185 employees and no women in the top tier at all. John Weiss would look at that. Did the company have any African Americans or Hispanics in their employ? Did they use any minority-owned vendors? Wait, said, Casey, what could this possibly have to do with Michelle's affair with Steve going sour? You don't want to know, one of the attorneys replied. Remind me tomorrow to ask about the talent you were using for the food commercials—was it representative of a diverse population? Asians, African Americans, Hispanics—did they have roles in the commercials? It's telling stuff. We'll explain it tomorrow.

TELLING STUFF
AND OTHER LEGAL DETAILS

The partners had just signed the biggest account in the history of the agency. They were gearing up to announce it publicly. It was a major coup. But they couldn't announce it now because they didn't have time. The attorneys needed them to provide details about the agency regarding both Steve and Michelle. The attorneys said there can be no surprises—good or bad. They needed to know everything. They might need to hire private investigators—probably a good idea for a few days.

Their human resources department was not familiar with how to handle a complaint of sexual harassment. The department staff didn't know how they were supposed to respond when it was reported. Dave Williams talked to Michelle as if she were a daughter instead of an employee. That was a bad move. The human resources department wasn't informed immediately. In fact, it didn't know for a couple of days that a report had been made. Although the department had never investigated a charge of sexual harassment, it knew that it was required by law to conduct a prompt and thorough investigation. The partners, human resources, and Steve Telleck found themselves in meetings regarding Michelle's charges for the better part of a week. Most of the business for these key executives was put on hold.

Michelle decided that she couldn't handle working there anymore. No one was talking to her. Steve wouldn't speak to her. Dave and Rich avoided her. The human resources staff corresponded with her only formally through memos that they "carbon-copied" to their corporate attorneys. She cried all night. Couldn't sleep. Couldn't keep her food down. She went to the doctor, and he gave her something for her nerves. It wasn't working. She called her attorney four days after she had reported Steve and said she didn't think she could come into work anymore. She wanted to resign. Could he help her write a letter of resignation? No, you can't leave right now, her attorney responded. You've got to stay where you are. It gives us leverage. The only way she could leave was if Steve was harassing her to the point that it was impossible to do her job. Her attorney called it a "constructive discharge" when an employee left a job because of serious and pervasive harassment and it was legally viewed as a dismissal since the resigning employee had no choice. But he knew she could tough this out. It will be worth it in the long run. Gives us more leverage in our negotiations.

Eight years and her job was over, she kept saying to her attorney. Couldn't he do something? She was drowning. No one was talking to her. Even those people she thought were her friends at work weren't saying anything more than they had to. The only one talking to her was

Rita, the production assistant. She wanted to have lunch with Michelle so she could hear all the details. Michelle knew that Rita didn't care about her—she just wanted the inside story, and the other employees were counting on Rita to get it for them. That's the way it had always been at the agency. Rita was the agency gossip. She always had the scoop, and usually most of it had a particle of truth to it. Michelle's attorney told Michelle these cases are never easy. Just keep holding on. It will be over before you know it.

Instead of having lunch with Rita, Michelle got in touch with Liz Anne, Nat Henderson's secretary. She got a lunch appointment with Mr. Henderson. He was good friends with her father and would always find time to meet with his friend's daughter. Besides, he thought, she works inside an agency he spends a lot of money with. It's always nice to check up on the people who are spending so much of your money on newspaper, television, and radio advertising. Nat told her to meet him at his club at noon the next day. Michelle met him and told him what was going on. She knew she shouldn't involve him because he was such good friends with the co-owners of Williams Casey. But she needed him to hear from her that if anything happened to her job, it wasn't because she was incompetent.

Nat was blown away by what she was telling him. All he could think of when she was talking was that he was glad it was his advertising agency this mess was happening to and not his own business. But the more he thought about it, the more he became convinced that it was indirectly happening to his business. Who at the agency was taking care of his business if they were all involved in this ordeal? And the more he thought about it, the more annoyed he became. These guys had handled this mess so sloppily. They were clumsy businessmen, and that wasn't good. And if this case went public, would he want his company associated with this agency? Chances are his company would be mentioned because some of the allegations occurred when Michelle and Steve were working on the Lake Farm Food account. Nat thought he needed to spend some time evaluating his future relationship with the Williams

Casey agency. The recent work he received from Williams Casey was great, but previously the stuff was ho-hum. Maybe it was time to shop around for another agency. It was time for an agency review, and it should be opened up to the other Chicago-based agencies. He was sure his director of advertising and marketing would agree with him. Things change, after all.

BACK AT THE RANCH

Meanwhile, Rich and Dave had seen better days as partners. Rich was very angry with Dave for the way he handled Michelle when she came in to complain. With the agency's lawyer billing over $400 an hour, just sorting out the complaint was going to cost the agency money. And their client acquisition announcement had to be delayed again, now because they didn't want to have any press contact at this point, just in case one of the other employees heard about all this. Who's he kidding? He's certain all the employees already know something is up. He needs to ask HR how to handle the employees on this. Then there is the insurance issue regarding liability coverage. At least the agency is covered, he reassured himself. Do they need to notify the insurance company? Rich wasn't sure whom he was more upset with—Michelle, Steve, or his partner of many years. They were going to have to settle this, and quickly.

Michelle met with her attorney. He needed to know what she wants. She wants to have things be the way they were before Steve arrived. She wants her shot at managing the Lake Farm Frozen Foods account. She wants her good standing within the agency back. Weiss told her there was no going back. She had to look at this from a different perspective. She was pursuing a legal resolution now. She cannot resolve her complaint in the family-type atmosphere of the old agency. Does she think she can stay there as an employee after this is over? It's a tough road. Most people find it very lonely, and relationships are so damaged that most people have no real future with the organization. On a personal note, he told her she should think about where she would like to go to work. Were there any other agencies she might like to go to, or maybe she would like to work on the client side. His goal was to get her a substantial cash settlement with outplacement, extended benefits, and so forth, but he couldn't rewrite history for her. Lawyers can't change human behavior. They can only make people accountable for what they have done. Think about what kind of damages (cash amount) would make her feel comfortable enough to move on from Williams Casey.

Michelle was despondent. She could hardly get into work. She stared at her computer screen for hours at a time. She hadn't been able to get anything done. The department was just working around her. She felt like the walking dead. Meanwhile, Steve had a burst of managerial energy. When he was around the office (he had been gone for long periods of time), he made it known to all the staff that he was in charge and it was his domain. He seemed to be on a major power surge. Michelle thought he was a disgustingly horrible person. She didn't know whom she disliked more—Steve or that spineless, self-centered man, Dave. How could she have been so wrong about him? And that worthless personnel director, Doreen? Her memos were making Michelle crazy. Today, she just got one from her that was obviously drafted by the company's attorney, saying that the company has a "zero tolerance" for sexual harassment and that it is taking her claim very seriously. Right—a month had passed, and the agency was just now sending her this memo! The agency executives have pretended that they are investigating her complaint when really it is all about lawyers now and protecting themselves. Michelle was no longer being treated as an employee. She was an enemy within. She was as welcome as an IRS agent in an accounting department. Her nerves couldn't take it, but Steve seemed unbothered. Why, she wondered. Have they assured him that she will break before she can really do damage? She was stronger than she looked, she told herself. If they ruined her career, they were going to pay for it, in every way she could think of.

Nat Henderson called Dave. He'd like to have lunch with both Dave and Rich—as soon as possible. Just a touch-base thing, he said. Dave and Rich didn't believe it.

The corporate attorneys called John Weiss. Let's schedule a settlement conference—an informal meeting. They have some facts on Weiss's client that he should know about—her employment record, her history of getting besotted with men she works with, clients, etc. Fine, Weiss said. He has some information on Steve Telleck, too. Weiss hung up. He's very satisfied with the fact that he was able to find out that Telleck had a previous brush with sexual harassment early on in his career. It had cost the newspaper he once worked for $6,500 to make something go away. At the time, the people he worked for kept it quiet because they weren't exactly good corporate citizens either. It was a great negotiating card. He could establish a pattern and practice on this guy. Michelle had a fabulous case, and it would be easy money when it came to attorney fees. No contest, no court case required.

Williams Casey's attorneys also felt like they had something. The second year Michelle had worked at the agency she had dated a guy named Nick from an auto dealer's association the agency represented. Nick was engaged at the time. It turned out to be a real mess. To this day, Nick says that he only had a few thoughtless times with Michelle, but she made out like it was a huge relationship. She was really angry when he dumped her. Everyone at the auto dealer's association knew about the triangle, and Nick had made it really clear that he hadn't been the aggressor; Michelle had been. The attorneys knew that in reality this Nick character sounded like a real sleaze; but, nonetheless, Michelle had gotten involved with a client and there was a lot of noise that followed. It supported Steve's story that she was upset with him that he dumped her. It showed a pattern.

Rich met with human resources. He questioned why they had ever made Doreen personnel director? Did she even know anything about this issue? She was painfully slow at the draw, and she was driving him crazy. If she had been proactive on all this sexual harassment and discrimination stuff, he wouldn't be upset now. No, the agency wouldn't be in the middle of this mess. He might get rid of her when this was all over. She's worthless. Apparently she doesn't know how to handle a sexual harassment investigation, and she's whining about the fact that the agency didn't budget for her to have any additional training on these issues. Yes, he knew that she had been turned down to go to a couple of conferences. Water over the dam now.

Doreen told him that employees have been talking to her about the problem between Steve and Michelle. People were complaining that Steve is never there, Michelle doesn't work, and the gossip is creating a terrible atmosphere in which to work. A couple of female employees left a letter under her door saying that this is all about the sexist men at the agency always doing things their way. The agency is destroying Michelle to save their old-boy team that now included Steve and Michael. Shame on Dave and Rich, they said. They didn't respect their owners. The letter was typed, said Doreen. It could have been written by anyone.

And there was more, Doreen went on. Tom, one of the guys in the creative department, said that his wife had been getting anonymous calls from some woman. The caller said that Tom's wife should know that he was fooling around with the office "ho"—Michelle Robertson. Tom was very upset about it because he had been strictly friends with Michelle for years. Who would do this? he had asked Doreen. But he didn't want to be involved in any of this taking-sides thing. Tom feels that the department is already divided. Some of the women support Michelle; others think she is a troublemaker—pretty and from a rich family. They always hated her. Now they have a good reason to show it. The men are keeping their distance, and some are acting like they are in a Steven Segal movie and standing guard for both Michael and Steve. Tom says that the department is in shambles. They even screwed up getting the one-day sale dubs out to the television and radio stations the other night. Fortunately, they made it, but they had never made such a last-minute error before. It almost cost the client $250,000 and the agency 15 percent of that. Tom wants to know when this is going to be over. Doreen ended by saying the attorneys were being miserable about the way they were requesting employee information. It was making her feel very uncomfortable. They were going into things she felt weren't appropriate. She wasn't sure how much experience they had.

Nat Henderson met with the partners and let them know that their business was up for grabs and that they would have to repitch the account for the first time in ten years. Nat assured them it was just an internal decision, a way of being fair with vendors the company does business with—it had nothing to do with Williams Casey and the quality of the agency's work. The presentations would be scheduled within sixty days. The RFPs to the other agencies were going out shortly.

The attorneys called and said that a settlement conference was scheduled for Friday. The partners needed to decide how much they would be willing to settle for if it looked as though Michelle would settle the suit now. They wanted to offer her an "exit package," make her sign a release, and have her agree to confidentiality regarding the settlement. The agency, on behalf of Steve, would admit no wrongdoing ever. According to the employee records, Michelle was making $87,000. They thought they would offer her $45,000 and extend her benefits for six months. Run it by your partner and accountant. Need to get a sexual policy distributed, too, once this was over. No need to reprimand or investigate Steve if this settles, *but* nothing like this should happen again.

Michelle's lawyer was hoping to get her $150,000 plus his fees. The other side started at $35,000. Weiss laughed and hinted that Steve has been through this before. He could tell the other lawyers didn't know that. He talked about Michelle's future and the fact that she had a flawless record at Williams Casey. She had even been promised the job Michael was doing. And Michael was making almost $200,000 now. Wasn't there a bit of a pay descrepancy at Williams Casey? Steve was at almost $300,000. Michelle hadn't hit $100,000. She lost her opportunity to go forward. Her reputation was damaged, and it could take her years to get her career back on track. John Weiss asked for $500,000 plus benefits, outplacement, and attorney fees. Furthermore he asked that the company discipline the obvious offender. Acknowledge that he harassed Michelle. Be accountable. This case could cost over a million in court. Save some money and settle. No policy in place. They were screwed. Face it.

The settlement broke down. Williams Casey's attorneys were unprepared to hear about Steve. They didn't even go into Michelle's background. No one made a move to reschedule a conference. They retreated. John Weiss felt good. He wanted damages to amount to Steve Telleck's wages plus all the extras. He wasn't going to take less than $400,000 for this case. The court in Illinois had good judges for these civil matters. A jury would award Michelle money once he really built the case that Steve was a jerk when it came to managing women who worked for him. He needed to get him checked out at the last place he worked. There had to be something there.

Bingo! Steve had had an affair with a married coworker. The woman was now a principle at one of the city's premiere agencies. She was the head of everything in the ad business. If her name was dragged into this, all hell would break loose in the advertising community. That was a bigger card than his first one. It wasn't anything that would mean all that much in court, but it was great material for settlement discussion. Steve would be begging his employer to settle. He'd probably throw some money in himself, he'd be so eager to settle it.

THE FINALE

Another settlement conference was rescheduled for two weeks before the agency had to present to its old client Lake Farm Foods. Michelle was not involved in the pitch, yet in the entire creative department, she had the most knowledge about the client. Steve had little, and Michael had less. Steve and Michael pulled people from other accounts to get some fresh ideas. Dave realized he had to step back in and wear his old creative director hat for this one. They could not lose a $20 million account. If they lost it, they would lose a huge chunk of their billing and would have to lay several people off. It would also send waves through the advertising agency business that Williams Casey had lost its touch. Old clients leaving was a very bad sign for business. They had to fight to keep this business.

Williams Casey's attorneys asked both co-owners to get on a conference call. They couldn't find much else about Michelle. They had nothing else to throw at John Weiss and his legal team. They were concerned about Steve's background though. They had reason to believe that there was something to what her attorney was saying about his being in trouble on this issue before. They could fight this present claim because no one saw anything, but it would be tough to make Michelle seem delusional if it happened before, much the same way. They needed to come up with a number to make this go away. Dave and Rich needed to think about a quarter of a million dollars just for her.

At 5:30 p.m. Rich got a call from the newspaper. It was Ron Davis, the business editor, who often called for quotes regarding advertising and marketing in the food or advertising business. He told Rich that a lot of rumors were flying about that some sort of sexual assault had occurred at the agency. Ron said that one of the city editors wanted to track the story and had come to Ron about it. That's why he was calling—was there an assault? Rich answered that there was absolutely nothing out of the ordinary. It was just a situation where one of the employees was concerned about her promotion and overreacted to her supervisor's decision to not promote her. Well, he had heard it was Michelle Robertson, said Ron, and that knowing her over the years, it didn't sound like her. Well, he was surprised too, said Rich, realizing, too late that he had given the identity of the complainant away. Are you going to fight it? We deny it because it didn't happen. So of course we are going to fight it. Gotta go, Ron. Talk to you soon.

The next Monday, John Weiss was surprised but not at all upset when he opened the paper and saw the big headline saying "Sexual Misconduct at Ad Agency Denied by Founder: Female Employee

Charges Williams Casey with Harassment." The city editor had called Weiss to verify that he was representing Michelle in an employment matter. Weiss didn't tell the editor what he was representing her for, but apparently Rich got caught by the newspaper. Someone had mailed the complaint to the newspaper, and Weiss was in the dark about who did it. It probably was scooped up off one of the desks at Williams Casey. Well, Michelle would be very upset, but at least now we would get action, one way or another. Unless the other side felt like it lost its incentive to settle because the press had already gotten a hold of it.

Michelle was mortified that her claim had gone public. But the more she thought about it, the more content she was about her original decision to report it. She got a call from two different women's groups. If she needed help, give them a call. A syndicated columnist called and asked to talk. Nat Henderson called her father. He was very sorry about this happening to Michelle. He thought she was a fine young woman. This was terrible. Michelle was sick of Steve and tired of everyone in her department. She carried herself differently the next day when she went into work. She was very comfortable about her decision to report that jerk, Steve. The hell with everyone.

The settlement was postponed. John Weiss couldn't make it. He had another trial going on. He asked to reschedule it the day before the Lake Farm Foods pitch. Dave Williams was frantic, but they had to get it over with before that meeting. He knew that most clients wouldn't care if a sexual harassment claim was pending. But Nat Henderson would. He was a gentleman, he had ethics, and he had a long-time friendship with Mac Robertson, Michelle's father.

OK, let the counteroffers go up to $250K, David and Rich said. Mentally they figured out that the whole thing was going to cost them almost $500,000 anyway. They had to pay Michelle, pay all the attorneys, get a sexual harassment program into effect, and replace Michelle (they would never find someone who would take her salary—they would have to offer more). And they were probably going to have to do some pro bono woman's stuff to let the community know that they weren't a bunch of male chauvinists. But they needed to get this behind them.

Michelle was hard to settle with—she wanted a justice they didn't want to consider. They should reprimand Steve in a visible way. That would show others that what he did was wrong and it would cost him (not just the company) something that was important to him.

The settlement talks went in Michelle's favor. She got $350,000 and benefits for a year. The company was required to sign a decree that it would institute a sexual harassment program. The agency didn't agree to reprimanding Steve, but John told Michelle that it would do something to him, especially after spending over $500,000 on the claim. Michelle was to leave the agency. But she had just secured a new job that she hadn't told anyone about yet. Within a month, she was going to the client side. She had been hired on as the new ad director for Lake Farm. Luckily the ad director was moving out of the area and the slot was open. Dave and Rich didn't know that until after they had done their presentation for Lake Farm Foods. They lost a major portion of their business, getting only the regional direct-mail business, and losing all electronic media for which they got 15 percent of everything they placed. By the end of the year, Williams and Casey decided to split up the agency. Williams along with Steve took over Golden Grocer, and Casey took the rest of the agency's business and stayed in Chicago. Casey had hated the fact that Williams had wanted to stand by Telleck. He had wanted to throw him out of the agency. It wasn't the sexual harassment claim that had ended their partnership; it was a lot of philosophical differences. The case, and what it had cost them, just happened to be the last straw.

Michelle felt very bruised from everything that had happened but loved her new job with her old client. Nat Henderson had been great, and it was wonderful work. She had lost some of her confidence in her work but hoped it would return in time. She knew there was still a great deal of gossip about her, but she was hopeful that someday it would die down a little. Meanwhile she just had to keep working hard and hope that her work would speak for her in ways that she couldn't.

Doreen left the agency business all together, still disgusted that the agency had never taken her warnings about sexual harassment seriously. She didn't want to work for any more start-up companies. She was going with a more established company that valued the human resources function.

CHAPTER 7

Executive Sex

Are there different rules for those at the top?

Y ou can tell a company by the men it keeps.

—W. A. Clarke

EQUAL EXPOSURE

"I will never forget the day my case made the paper. It was the worst and best day of my life. I was so tired of my former employer's mocking indifference to what had happened to me. When I saw the article in print, not only did I feel stronger and better about my decision to speak up, but I knew, for the first time since all this had begun, that my former company had to start being accountable for what my ex-boss, the CEO of the company, had done to me. When I had first reported him to the board, it seemed like they did everything they could to protect him and expose me. I felt like a nothing. Once it was all out in the open, not only did I feel relieved, but I felt like I had been given validation by people I didn't even know. I chose to believe that some people reading the article would have the same sense of outrage that I had when I experienced it. I felt as though I had some power against someone who had once had so much power over me. Although I was out of a job and possibly out of a career, I felt better about myself than I had in two years. Once and for all, he was exposed, and he deserved it!"

Laura, 35,
Former director of marketing for a
telecommunications company

Perhaps one of the most interesting behavior patterns regarding sexual misconduct in the workplace is the way companies have dealt with charges against senior-level people, particularly CEOs. Privy to the discussions of board members agonizing over the future of their organizations or the careers of their CEOs, I see more emotion and anguish that is often absent when sexual harassment in the organization occurs elsewhere. It is taken so personally, by otherwise so terribly professional people, that I often am taken aback by their strong emotions. "Arthur is such a wonderful man, I couldn't sleep last night." "I am sick over this. I am just devastated." "I wish I could do something for him." "I've had the hardest time believing that there is this other side to him." "I just wonder what he has been going through," etc.

When I deliver an official report about what the conduct was and what conclusions have been arrived at, the members of the board believe the results but they can't understand the motivation behind the behavior. It almost paralyzes them for a moment, and they are very lost about what the next steps might be—and if they can handle making them.

A case in point: A couple of years ago, two male employees accused the CEO of their company of creating a sexually hostile environment for all employees. According to these employees, their CEO was sleeping with various lower-status employees and using them to play out his sexual fantasies. This was a side of him that neither his wife, nor his children, nor the board of directors knew about until now. The men didn't report the sexual misconduct. They simply planted evidence that the board couldn't ignore. Apparently the CEO restricted his extramarital affairs to work, and he enjoyed taking photographs of them inside hotel rooms he rented for these affairs. He kept his photographs in a file in his desk, and one of his employees came across them looking for something while the CEO was traveling. This employee couldn't resist showing them to someone who happened to dislike the CEO. The photos were clumsily photocopied and shown to the board, the employees, and some outside vendors of the company.

The board was forced to respond. The board members were sick at heart at the sexual misconduct they uncovered as a result of the photographs (and they were the tip of the iceberg), but still they couldn't make themselves dismiss the CEO. Instead they felt closer to him, sorry for him. They felt like their beloved brother had sinned. And instead of being offended that he had sinned in their own backyard, they grappled with the question of what could have possibly driven their friend, a member of their team, to such dangerous behavior. It was one of *them* that "it" was happening to, and they were devastated. Please help them figure out a way to solve this, they pleaded, so that no one gets hurt. He's too good of a manager. Without him, we just don't think we would have such a well-run organization.

In this case, against all recommendations made to them by outside counsel, myself included, they did *not* fire the CEO. He got counseling. Actually, though, the bonding between the board members and the CEO hasn't lasted. As time has gone on, some have experienced individual and quiet resentment over what he put their organization through. They are amazed that it didn't make the news. The organization came dangerously close to damaging its corporate reputation. And they know, without question, that they lost the respect of many of their ethical employees. The employees knew what was going on, and they knew the board didn't do anything about it. It was clear to the employees that there were different rules for management.

And now, for another CEO story: Recently, a lawyer representing a large, privately held corporation called asking if I had any ideas about what to do with a CEO who habitually sexually harassed the women who work for him. Having been charged numerous times with sexual harassment, he was sent to extensive counseling to correct his ways. Within days of returning from off-site counseling for both sexual misconduct and alcohol abuse, he had grabbed at the breasts of a new employee who had entered his office. While stories like this are not common, they are hardly unusual, unfortunately.

A FALL FROM GRACE
AND OTHER TALES OF 1995

Looking back at the past decade, I would choose 1995 as the most interesting year in terms of CEOs caught in the public spotlight with sexual harassment charges pinned on them. From W. R. Grace & Company, to the head of a hospital in New York, to the CEO of Del Laboratories,

CEOs were taking the heat—and some got burned, or at least lost their jobs. And some just got richer and remained in power.

A GOLDEN PARACHUTE BREAKS THE FALL

In 1995 J. P. Bolduc resigned from his position as chief executive of W. R. Grace, a $5 billion company. A joint statement issued by Bolduc and the company stated that the reasons for his sudden departure from the company stemmed from "differences of style and philosophy." But there seemed to be another story behind the resignation, one that was an internal affair.

In a *New York Times* story, Diana Henriques reported that a draft of W. R. Grace's preliminary proxy statement said:

On February 28, 1995, Judge Tyler reported to the Board that grounds existed to find that Mr. Bolduc had sexually harassed certain employees of the Company. Mr. Bolduc vigorously denied, and continues to deny, that he engaged in any such misconduct. In light of the report from Judge Tyler, the Board, and Mr. Bolduc mutually determined that Mr. Bolduc's employment should be terminated on negotiated terms. . . .

Henriques writes in the same article:

The case appears to be the first time that a major American corporation has cited sexual harassment complaints as the explanation for a chief executive's resignation, said several women's advocacy groups. As such it puts even the most powerful executives on notice that, under certain circumstances, even disputed allegations of harassment can cost them their jobs, although in this case it did not cost Mr. Bolduc his generous severance package.

In a public statement by his attorney, Bolduc, married and the father of four children, "absolutely, categorically, unequivocally and vehemently denies that he ever engaged in any act of sexual harassment." And in defense of Bolduc, at the time of his departure certain power struggles were going on in the company's executive offices related to retaliation for Bolduc's disclosure of Grace family practices regarding consulting deals and perquisites. These fights, some say, contributed to the "mudslinging" directed at Bolduc. However, what was undisputed was that Harold Tyler, a retired judge, did act as an adviser to the board, interviewed five individual females regarding sexual misconduct by Bolduc, and, according to one director, "found the witnesses valid and their claims credible and well-corroborated."

HOSPITAL PRIVILEGES

Bolduc had the distinction of being the first CEO that year to face the public embarrassment of being linked to sexual misconduct in his workplace. However, right on the heels of that scandal followed another involving the CEO of a hospital agency. He too was accused of sexual harassment, and he too denied it. But he also resigned just a few days after a hospital employee filed the complaint. Although he was accused of having made "unwanted requests for dinner dates, late night phone calls and inappropriate messages on e-mail," the incidents did not involve any allegations of physical contact. The hospital had retained a law firm to investigate the claims of sexual harassment, but the investigation was only two weeks into it when the doctor resigned. His resignation came just forty-eight hours after the preliminary report had been delivered to the board.

WASSONG STRIKES A SOUR NOTE

Meanwhile, still in 1995, women working at Del Laboratories on Long Island, in New York, went after the CEO of their company, with the help of the EEOC and an attorney from the organization 9 to 5. Their suit turned out to be the EEOC's largest successful sexual harassment case to date. Dan Wassong was a refugee from pre-World War II Poland. He was reported to have come to the United States in the early 1950s. He was named president of Del in 1969, four years after joining the company. He was named chairman in 1992. In 1995, at the time the settlement with the EEOC was reached, he was reported to be earning $1.58 million and owned 35 percent of the company's stock.

Jonneigh Adrion, an administrative assistant to Wassong, led a group of both current and former employees of Wassong to the EEOC door with claims of sexual harassment by the man who in many circles of power was thought of as influential and charming. The EEOC filed a lawsuit against Del in 1994 on behalf of over a dozen women who claimed that Wassong had sexually harassed them during their employment at the company. In fact, Adrion described one incident in which Wassong just reached out and grabbed her left breast while she was going over his calendar with him. Another employee, Lucy Pelligrino, said that Wassong told her that her voice irritated him and that he didn't want her to open her mouth. He did, though, according to her claim, want something else. Pelligrino said that at a formal company meeting, he led her from a conference into another room and told her something important was in his pocket and that he wanted her to reach in and take it out. Fearful of his reaction, Pelligrino said she did what she was told but experienced self-loathing for complying with the CEO's sexual request.

All the social and professional power held by a man described as having one of the richest social lives from Manhattan to Southampton, didn't match the determination and strength of the women banded together by a twenty-two-year old assistant who felt that they had been wronged. Like the Dabney Coleman character in the movie 9 to 5, Wassong met his match in the women who had served as his support staff. Thirty-four women in all were lined up and ready to testify against Wassong when lawyers for Del Laboratories agreed to settle the case in

August 1995 for $1.185 million, to be divided up among the fifteen official complainants. The EEOC also required Del to establish a toll-free number for employees to report sexual harassment to an outside party or counsel and to conduct harassment training for all its 1,200-plus employees. The settlement also stipulated that the chief executive officer undergo one-on-one training. Although a substantial amount of money, the settlement was still less that what Wassong earned in one year. Wassong and Del Laboratories did not admit to any wrongdoing and publicly, through their public relations spokesperson, said that they settled "to avoid the continued distraction of senior management in defending against the false accusations and the burden of protracted litigation." At the time of the settlement, the board acknowledged that Wassong would remain with the company.

THE MELODY LINGERS ON

One of the most controversial CEOs in regard to sexual harassment accusations is the founder of ICN Pharmaceuticals, Milan Panic, who has faced various sexual harassment charges since at least as far back as 1990. Interestingly, stock performance has soared as allegations of misconduct continue to mount. Undisputed is that Panic, prime minister of Yugoslavia in 1993, is deemed as one of the most successful leaders in the pharmaceutical industry, having built over a $3 billion company with stock that outperforms any other in the drug industry. But according to his general counsel, being king does have its price. Although Panic has been hit with suits from over six different former and present employees, and although the company and Panic have come up with millions of dollars to settle most of these cases, both the board and loyal insiders feel that Panic is merely a target of women looking for money from a powerful, larger-than-life, successful man.

In 1998, *U.S. News & World Report* reported that Panic, although facing two harassment suits, was given a $1.8 million bonus in addition to his regular salary of $644,680. The claims against the sixty-nine-year-old executive have had a similar ring to them, although loyal Panic fans say that is because there has been a conspiratorial effort of sorts. In 1996, Panic himself paid out $3.6 million to settle a case brought against him by Debra Levy in 1995. Levy alleged that Panic demanded sex from her soon after she began to work for him as his secretary. In her allegations she also acknowledges that she complied. When she began to refuse him, she claims that her work responsibilities were diminished and she was terminated. Levy also raised the issue of a paternity suit regarding the son she gave birth to during her "compliance" period with Panic.

Other women with complaints against Panic also reported M.O.'s similar in sound to that described by Levy. Claims ranged from Panic telling several of the claimants that they had perfect bodies for making love, allegedly groping them in elevators, groping them under the table during business meetings, and saying that he wanted to "make a baby."

- In 1993 Colleen James, a trade show manager, alleged that Panic repeatedly propositioned her and said he loved her and that she had the perfect body for making love. The company settled with James but required her to sign a confidentiality agreement.

- In January 1995 Debra Levy filed suit, and the company and Panic settled the case in 1996.

- In 1995 Dawn Zika, of the customer service department, alleged that Panic was harassing her and that his driver was calling her to arrange dates. Zika filed a suit with the state of California, and ICN settled.

- In 1996 former human resources executive Martinelli filed suit against Milan Panic and the company.

- In 1996 Michelle McKenney, an executive secretary, also filed a lawsuit. She too alleged that she had been groped and grabbed by Panic and said that one of his sexual invitations to her was to "make a baby together."

PANIC'S PANACHE OR POWER GRIP?

For several years ICN has found itself caught in a situation where its greatest strength in corporate power is its greatest liability when it comes to issues of personal ethics and accountability—in a word, Panic. Those defending Panic's position claim he is a victim of greedy women going after a powerful, even generous, man and find certain facts to support Panic's "poor me, I'm powerful, what am I gonna do with all these chicks that are after me" excuses. But I know many powerful men in similar executive positions who do not have women suing them for sexual harassment. These men also have enemies, and have had to fire people, demote them, etc., but they *do not* have a string of million-dollar lawsuits to settle before every annual shareholder's meeting. Rather than dealing with the root problem, ICN seems only willing to stem the effects as they crop up.

ICN is not alone. Many companies believe that the way to "manage" sexual harassment claims in their workplace is to stave off these personal attacks one by one. One executive at another company did not want anyone but top management trained on sexual harassment. What are we going to teach them—how to do a witch-hunt? he asked wryly. Why don't we just have the EEOC come in and teach them the ropes on how to sue us? Believe it or not, some companies do not educate their employees on their rights as workers because the companies think it will encourage lawsuits. And so training does not take place because of fear of lawsuits. Based upon my experience, some companies will receive minor inquiries, not claims, after a companywide harassment training program. Employees, knowingly or not, will test the grievance procedure system to find out whether it is real. But I've never been involved with a companywide program that has prompted a lawsuit. Some companies may have already had a suit, or may have had a suit pending, but no one has misread a training effort as an opportunity to launch a suit.

It is my feeling that the employees are respectful of the company's efforts and realize that the core of the program is about the company respecting their rights. No organization is perfect, and that includes both management and workers. But together they are trying to do things better. Companies like ICN have not delved into the real problem. The environment for both men and women in these companies isn't about openness and fairness. Instead, it is about containment and perhaps a different set of rules for those who make the place profitable. What is so troublesome about all this is that it misses the whole point of sexual harassment law. The idea was to protect people from those misusing their power to obtain sex from those who had so much to lose if they refused to comply.

"CATEGORICALLY" MORE

In 1997, a pharmaceutical company agreed to an almost $10 million settlement for claims that its president and other executives pressured women employees for sex and replaced older workers with young and beautiful women. This settlement surpassed Del Laboratories' settlement, thus becoming the largest one ever reached by the Equal Employment Opportunity Commission. The EEOC charged former Astra AB CEO Lars Bildman, along with other Astra officials, with replacing mothers and older female employees with beautiful, young single women whom they would pressure to have sex with them. Some of the employees claimed Bildman had fondled them, and some said he demanded that eight hours of work be followed by eight hours of drinking and partying.

In early 1996 *Business Week* magazine notified Boston-based Astra USA that the magazine was about to release the shocking results of a six-month investigation regarding widespread sexual misconduct at the Swedish-owned, Boston-based pharmaceutical company. *Business Week* had engaged in an extensive investigation, one that would probably more than match the competency of an investigation conducted by a skilled and experienced legal investigator. The magazine had interviewed over seventy employees and uncovered a pattern of sexual

LETTING GO OF THE CEO—
WHY IT'S SO TOUGH TO SAY GOOD-BYE

- **The value of the CEO versus the value of the other employee.** Although it sounds harsh, boards have wrestled with the problem of letting go of their most valuable asset instead of the accusing employee, who could easily be replaced tomorrow.

- **The CEO and the company's image are one and the same.** The person most responsible for building the company has his or her prints all over the image of the company, from the product to the media. Without this particular CEO, the top spot, even if immediately filled, will seem empty in terms of recognition and image.

- **Business reasons.** The company is doing well, and the person running it is responsible for its success. The company can't afford to change the formula. Business will suffer greatly with any top management change. Besides, succession is a problem. There is no time to consider the best replacement. And the management change doesn't seem to be on the company's terms.

- **The CEO's achievements.** The CEO has done a tremendous job running the company. The CEO's performance has made everyone money. *It seems totally unfair to release this person.*

- **Financial reasons.** A sudden change in leadership could send the wrong message to shareholders, employees, customers, and the public. *But then, again, so could allowing a known offender to remain at the top of an organization.*

- **The invitation for exposure.** When a CEO is asked to step down as the result of a sexual harassment claim, it invites everyone—the media and the public—into a company.

misconduct that took the definition of both quid pro quo and hostile work environment to an almost unreal example of just how bad—just how awful—the behavior can be. At the center of it, and in fact leading the sexual harassment, was the forty-nine-year-old Bildman. At the time he met up with *Business Week,* Bildman had been CEO of Astra USA Inc. for fifteen years. According to *Business Week's* own report:

> *Business Week* had found a dozen cases of women who claimed that they were either fondled or solicited for sexual favors by Bildman or other executives. Many women described evenings in which they were expected to escort senior executives to bars and dancing clubs. Others received frequent invitations to join the often inebriated managers in their hotel suites for more intimate late-night gatherings. Until recently, company parties were raucous affairs at which heavy drinking and dancing were virtually mandated. "Guys were encouraged to get as drunk as they could—and do whatever they could to the women," recalls Kimberley A. Cote, a former Astra sales rep who obtained an out-of-court settlement of harassment charges in 1994. "If they felt like grabbing a woman by the boob or by the ass, that was O.K."

The company admitted to allowing a hostile work environment—including requests for sexual favors in exchange for favorable treatment. Bildman, who was fired by Astra in 1996 and then sued for $15 million for misuse of company funds for high-priced prostitutes, home repairs, and other personal pleasures, said, "I categorically deny that there was any pattern of sexual harassment at Astra."

CHAPTER 8

Corporations Looking for the Quick Fix

Is there one?

No snowflake in an avalanche ever feels responsible.

—Stanislaw Lec

THE HOUR OF CRISIS

Whether a company's intentions are honorable or not, it is always best to resolve a sexual harassment claim as quickly as possible. The longer the cap is off the bottle, the more the toxic fumes caused by the problem are able to spread throughout the company. An out-of-control claim can cause serious damage in a matter of hours, certainly substantial damage if it continues on for days, weeks, or even months. But those companies that depend on the quick-fix method of settling each claim of harassment, one at a time, misuse the settlement resolution process as an overall way to fix all their deeper discrimination problems.

About four years ago, I spoke with a senior executive who worked for a high-profile financial company that was having severe problems with sexual harassment at every turn. A company with locations in almost every state, it had been averaging two serious claims per office per year. Up to that point, the company thought it was managing the problem and still preserving the way its male-dominated corporate culture worked. After all, the company was profitable, so settling sexual harassment claims without thinking about the troubling message behind the stream of complainants was its way of dealing with discrimination.

But it seemed that settling claims was finally taking a toll on the company beyond the financial exit packets for the offended. It seemed that the women complaining of sexual harassment were different, more confident. And men within the organization were offended by the actions of other men within the offices in which they worked. The culture the company was trying to keep was changing from within. Finally, when it looked as though the company was about to face a class-action suit organized by a known plaintiff attorney, it realized it was no longer able to "dismiss" claims or the bigger problem behind those claims. The previous "make it, make her, go away" one-by-one settlement strategy failed to contain anyone or anything. The company, having never addressed the two main problems—operating without any women in management and failing to implement any real policy on discrimination—had hit a point where it had no choice but to do both. Entering late into the responsible-employer arena, it had a lot to learn. Even though it would still have preferred to go back to the old days, reality made it quite clear that the quick fix no longer worked there.

WHY COMPANIES HOPE FOR A QUICK FIX

There are a number of reasons why companies grasp at quick-fix methods to address sexual misconduct in the workplace, and not all of those reasons are wrong. In fact, some of the reasons why they choose to handle claims swiftly with a settlement are both thoughtful and sound:

- To minimize disruption to the business. Claims take away people and resources from the core of the business.

- To protect the company's reputation. Many claims are not worth the cost of a public match. Companies are very disadvantaged these days when it comes to what a claim gone public can do to their reputation.

- To protect employees from invasive inquiries and from outsiders scrutinizing an environment that the company feels belongs to the employees.

- To save money. Defending oneself from a claim takes substantial financial resources for legal counsel, public relations counsel, and the settlement sum itself. Many businesses feel they can cut their losses early.

- To protect a "valuable" senior executive from exposure. When a CEO or senior-level person is charged with sexual harassment, the company has to think differently about its strategy. The CEO and the company's image and reputation are almost always one and the same. That joint image must be considered.

- To protect the company from being exposed as a bad employer. As a claim unfolds publicly, more information about the way a company does business, from the inside, gets to customers.

- To protect the board from liability issues. Corporate boards today are extremely concerned about their own liability when it comes to discrimination cases. When a claim comes to the attention of the board of a company, I always find that company management, which until then wouldn't address the problem, will begin to act more swiftly when the board starts calling the shots.

- To protect a company from the EEOC. If claims are settled early, the complainants may not have gone to the EEOC yet. When employees have tapped into an agency in the state or federal system for help to resolve their employee issues, the agency, particularly the EEOC, may go after the company with bigger charges of discrimination.

WHY AN EMPLOYEE
MAY HOPE FOR A QUICK FIX

When companies are faced with an internal dispute over sexual harassment and haven't invested much time or thought in addressing such issues, they often find they don't have many options available to them except to settle. They don't have any confidence in themselves or in any of their resolution channels, if, in fact, there are any. In situations like this, the claim may very well be one that could have easily been resolved early on, within the company, without incident, and with little cost.

Unfortunately, many companies have to settle claims that are without merit and are just plain weak. It is a painful process for companies and their legal counsel to just "take the hit" and settle when they feel someone is taking advantage of a law that is in place to protect workers.

SO IS THERE SUCH A THING AS A QUICK FIX?

The answer is no. The quick-fix solutions in sexual harassment cases really amount to handling each claim one at a time. But there inevitably comes a point, or a difficult case, that forces companies and their employees to view the issue of sexual harassment as being much more than a series of annoying complaints. Multiple complaints are a sign of a bigger issue that needs to be addressed. The longer a company waits to address the core of the crisis, the more costly it will be for all involved.

I was asked to consult with a company that had three different complaints, all substantiated, within the period of a year. They were all against the same high-level person. The claims cost the company what it termed "pocket change," a quarter of a million dollars each. The person accused was bringing so much revenue into the company that those who complained were deemed unimportant and easy to throw away. But the company, like many start-ups, wanted to go public; and investors, particularly venture capitalists, don't like liabilities within an organization. In this particular situation, the company kept the high-liability manager, but changed his role, stripping him of most of his management responsibilities. He remained as a revenue producer and in the field. Personally, I still believe he is a liability and that story hasn't ended. I have always found that major investors are extremely helpful in voicing ethical concerns about companies that have automatically used the quick-fix way to address employee problems. They don't like it. They don't want to be putting their money into companies that continue to act irresponsibly. They ask that companies get up to speed in the area of corporate responsibility and develop internal programs that address discrimination and diversity issues in a manner that meets today's standards.

CHAPTER 9

Foreign Affairs

The sexual culture clash collides

with international businesses

The global warning on sexual harassment heard around the world: the Japanese automaker, the American plant workers, and the $34 million sexual harassment lesson on U.S. civil rights.

In March 1998, Mitsubishi Motor Manufacturing of America, known in auto maker circles as MMMA, settled for $34 million with the Equal Employment Opportunity Commission. This settlement ended, at least legally, what is probably the most globally publicized claim of sexual harassment against any company, U.S or international. (I do need to be specific by saying *company*, because Paula Jones's claim against then Governor, now President, Clinton, continues to lead the media frenzy race in alleged sexual misconduct in the workplace.) To date, the landmark settlement by Mitsubishi stands alone as being the largest sexual harassment settlement agreement ever reached, not only in the United States, but in the world. More significant than this distinction, I believe, is that this case brought forth one of the most complicated dilemmas regarding civil rights law protecting workers in the American workplace. When it comes to sexual attitudes and the workplace, the working world isn't even close to finding common ground.

A WORLD APART

Forget for a moment what Japanese or European companies may think of our laws regarding sexual harassment. Hometown U.S. corporations need all the help they can get in finding their own way through U.S. laws—in being effective in managing human sexual behavior in the workplace and creating environments that are safe and healthy for all workers. What, then, must be happening to international companies doing business in the United States when it comes to interpreting U.S. civil rights and even murkier issues like defining unwanted sexual harassment versus supporting positive interaction between male and female coworkers?

Different cultures with different attitudes toward sexuality and women often spell different management styles and certainly different responses to claims of a sexually hostile environment. Those involved in the crisis at Mitsubishi, both management and the workers, have been able to point out to us some of the more glaring challenges that remain unsolved when it comes to finding a common global understanding in the area of gender equality on the job. Bridging cultural differences, specifically in the area of sexual behavior and the laws protecting U.S. workers, is now an essential part of doing business internationally. It is one that also leaves many companies just as open and vulnerable to lawsuits as Mitsubishi.

THE CLAIMS AGAINST MITSUBISHI

It took more than two years for Mitsubishi to reach an agreement with the EEOC, having been charged in early 1996 by the agency with violating Title VII of the Civil Rights Act of 1964 and the Civil Rights Act of 1991. The EEOC, the federal agency responsible for enforcing such civil rights laws, filed a class-action suit against the company on behalf of approximately 350 current and former female workers, claiming widespread sexual harassment and retaliation took place at the manufacturing facility since 1990. The claims of sexual misconduct were ugly, and, if true, a nightmare for anyone subjected to them.

THE UNIVERSAL LANGUAGE

The company settled with the EEOC in 1998; and a year earlier, in 1997, it settled a private suit with twenty-seven plaintiffs for about $9.5 million. Still, it has never admitted any wrongdoing. As with most settlements I have seen or been involved with, Mitsubishi's decision to remain silent in the "remorse department" is typical, common, and almost always a judgment call made for legal reasons. Because it was labeled a foreign company, its lack of compassion for its U.S. workers looked even more diabolical. For liability reasons, few companies like

Mitsubishi can or do say they are sorry for their actions or the behavior of their employees.

Yet I have found in my role as a third-party neutral in settlement negotiations that the personal need for an apology is the single most important settlement request made by female plaintiffs or complainants. Unfortunately, it doesn't often get heard by the wronged employees who have the emotional need to hear it. Usually they are left with the classic task of "moving on" without the people they once worked for ever acknowledging illegal workplace acts. Even when financial settlements are made, complainants often feel that a crime has gone unpunished and those who complained were bought out and dismissed as corporate nuisances rather than treated as valuable individual contributors.

To date, we have heard very little from the female workers who filed the private suits at Mitsubishi, but I suspect they were hoping their employer would work on ways to prevent sexual harassment from happening again, rather than ways to obtain good press for the company's very expensive recovery efforts. Because the EEOC and the attorneys representing those complainants in the private suits against Mitsubishi were able to settle for a record amount, money had to be the final word in this case, and, in fact, it was.

WHAT WENT WRONG AT MITSUBISHI?

I guess it would be too flip to answer the question about what went wrong at Mitsubishi by saying "everything." Still, in looking at the situation, I am tempted to conclude that almost everything that could go wrong did go wrong.

The name *Mitsubishi* signifies an enormous world power in many areas of international business. The automobile factory in Normal, Illinois, is a small portion of Mitsubishi's empire. The plant is an impressive facility, and from many viewpoints, it is a great place to work. I even thought so when I first saw it looming above the cornfields that surround it. When you see the plant, it doesn't seem out of line for American workers to be making Japanese cars in such a pleasant rural community. What does seem out of line is that such horrific behavior could have gone unchecked for so long.

Problems like those that Mitsubishi experienced can never be solved with a quick-fix action plan. Such problems grew over a long period of time and their roots are deep within the company's culture. In order for the proposed solutions to actually work, not only do the internal processes within the company need to change, but the culture needs to alter itself completely. Changing a company's culture is a long and slow process and is only as good as the management team leading the change.

BASIC BLUNDERS

Mitsubishi committed two giant blunders. One, according to the allegations by both the EEOC and the private suits, is that management did little or nothing to stop threatening and frightening verbal and physical sexual assaults from occurring right on the plant floor by both male managers and workers against female workers. Mitsubishi's biggest "other" notable blunder, which was pointed out by the media, is that the company actually paid for hundreds of workers' time and the buses that transported them to the doors of the EEOC to protest the agency's suit against their employer.

BASIC LESSONS

Although there was much publicity surrounding the suit, and for that matter, a great deal of criticism directed at Mitsubishi for how it handled matters once the suit was formally filed, it is my opinion that the real lessons to be learned from what happened in Normal, Illinois, unfortunately, remain with the employees.

Many look at the Mitsubishi situation as, if nothing else, a good case in crisis communications. Strictly from a public relations and employee relations perspective, I couldn't agree more. In fact, *PR News* in a November 3, 1997, article entitled "Mitsubishi Steers in Wrong Direction with Lawsuit" pointed out some critical mistakes that Mitsubishi appeared to have made that don't go far beyond what any public relations student learns in basic Public Relations 101. In its case study, the publication stated that three big lessons could be learned from the Mitsubishi case:

> Late is not better than never; with volatile issues like sexual harassment, you'd better show your caring side from the get-go, and don't wait for a lawsuit if you suspect something needs to change at your corporation.

But those points are only the beginning of what I believe we can learn from Mitsubishi Motors. There is no doubt in my mind that to fully analyze the entire Mitsubishi case from start to finish, about just what really happened, requires a separate book. And because of the importance of this case, it is very likely that someone will write one, though it won't be me. Despite the fact that I had firsthand experience with the Mitsubishi case and got to make some interesting observations, I still don't know enough about what exactly happened between workers. However, what I do know is that there are critical turning points in cases of sexual harassment that put companies and employees in positions that can change lives, bankrupt businesses, destroy organizations, and catapult a company into media orbit. And this case is one very good example.

THE MITSUBISHI TIME LINE

December 15, 1994
Twenty-nine women filed a federal lawsuit against Mitsubishi Motors Manufacturing of America for having a sexually hostile work environment.

April 9, 1996
The Equal Employment Opportunity Commission filed a class-action suit against MMMA on behalf of over 300 women at the Normal, Illinois, plant.

April 22, 1996
Mitsubishi assists 3,000 of its employees by paying for 59 buses to the Chicago office of the EEOC to protest the lawsuit. Top executives of Mitsubishi meet separately the same week to discuss strategy.

May 14, 1996
Mitsubishi hires Lynn Martin. It was later reported that Mitsubishi paid Martin more than $2 million to head a task force to study the company's internal systems and recommend changes.

February 12, 1997
Martin holds a press conference to announce the changes her independent consultants recommend.

August 28, 1997
Mitsubishi settles the private suits with twenty-seven of the twenty-nine women for $9.5 million.

October 1998
The personnel manager of Mitsubishi resigns after just six months on the job because, he noted, "I was being forced to participate in an event that I cannot ethically support." He was referring to a "seriously flawed P.R. strategy" he felt was being implemented to "rehabilitate Lynn Martin's reputation at the expense of the best interests" of the company as well as the morale of the company's employees.

June 10, 1998
Mitsubishi and the EEOC announce that they have settled the lawsuit brought by the EEOC for $34 million.

On the day the company had bused its employees to Chicago to protest the EEOC charges, I was meeting with company executives in another part of the city. I was one of a group of consultants asked to speak to approximately forty Mitsubishi officials who had gathered there. Top management was present from both Japan and the U.S. operations of Mitsubishi, as well as the company's public relations, public affairs, and in-house legal staffs. At that time, those of us who spoke to the officials encouraged them to ask for forgiveness and settle the case.

Mitsubishi Motor Sales of America (MMSA), a separate marketing and sales company based in California that markets the cars Mitsubishi makes, also encouraged the group to resolve the situation as quickly as possible. MMSA did not have a problem with sexual harassment within its organization, had a solid internal education and grievance program, and was concerned about the negative effects of this case. MMSA, being key in the retail distribution of consumer products in the United States, along with over 500 dealers, knew it would feel the impact of any negative publicity regarding the case. Later on, it was, in fact, MMSA and the dealers who had to face boycotts, deal with picketing by NOW, and respond to Jesse Jackson's concerns that they weren't doing all that they could for minorities. Soon, all subsidiaries of Mitsubishi in the United States were worried about the possible damage to their own divisions' reputations simply because they shared the same name. During those times, you couldn't tune into Leno or Letterman without their talking about Mitsubishi in their respective monologues. And each day the publicity just seemed to get worse.

Initially, I was asked to quietly work with MMSA and MMMA to help resolve the problems within the plant and assist the plant in moving forward as a more sensitive employer. But the company already had many outside voices advising it on what was needed, and the decision to hire a high-profile person was simultaneously recommended by outside consultants. Former Secretary of Labor Lynn Martin was hired by both MMSA and MMMA, and Martin and her former press aide from her days in D.C. set up camp at the plant and began a program that was called the Lynn Martin Initiative. Martin's team served as an "independent" third party, which unfortunately added one more group of opinions and people with agendas to an already divided house. Although it is just my own thought, I believe that Mitsubishi made its most serious mistake by handing control over to an outside entity. Although Japanese management was completely unprepared to handle the hammering it received from the media, the EEOC, special-interest groups, and some employees, it might have been better off if it took a crash course on sexual harassment and crisis communications and fended for itself.

WHAT WE CAN LEARN

- Recognize cultural differences within an organization. Culture clashes inside a workplace can cause serious internal and external damage to a company and its workers. In this case, management was primarily Japanese, and most of the workers were midwestern Americans. Management didn't know how to manage a crisis within the United States, let alone understand the complexities of U.S. civil law.

- Have universal, global standards within your company. Many employees of U.S. companies work and reside in other countries. Make it clear that these employees must operate under the standards set by the U.S. company. Some employees will take advantage of the overseas work atmosphere to leave behind acceptable workplace behavior practices. Companies should communicate to all employees that their workplace standards are to be upheld throughout their global workplace.

- Be aware that sexual harassment is truly a foreign phrase to many other cultures in our global working society. Many other countries do not understand Title VII law in the United States or the concept of unwanted sexual advances. Even the most basic concept behind sexual harassment law has been known to be misunderstood. One worker told me that he thought that when women at work told him no, they were just doing the expected—playing hard to get. He thought they were telling him to try harder.

- **Understand that the United States sends conflicting messages to other cultures.** We have strict rules in the workplace, but other cultures see strong sexual messages coming through our media, making it difficult to understand the difference between *workplace rules* and *American culture.*

- **Make sure that internal guidance given to foreign companies from U.S. executives is accurate.** This is actually a big problem. Foreign companies should not necessarily listen to Americans who work for them. The Americans may be just passing along their own bias and discriminatory practices to their management. The companies need to check with legal counsel.

- **Provide better resources to international companies doing business in the United States.** Understanding our civil laws is not easy for Americans, so it's not surprising that it's very tough for foreign workers. Not only do we need to make it easier to access information about the standards of the American workplace, but we need to make the information more understandable. (As a matter of fact this goes not only for foreign executives but for U.S. workers, too!) I recommend that international companies seek out global technology for educating themselves and their workers. Customized on-line training designed for both the company, its culture, its industry, and the places where it is doing business may be an effective way to reach workers and create a work environment that meets U.S. standards of civil law. International companies doing business in the U.S. must set up internal programs based upon the EEOC's recommendations and legal and professional counsel.

- **Create internal programs that can thrive in a global environment.** In addition to comprehending U. S. sexual harassment law, the next biggest challenge for international companies is being able to effectively communicate their policies and positions worldwide. Many companies have impressive programs implemented at corporate headquarters, but outposts live and work by their own rules—in some cases, that means none.

CHAPTER 10

The Sexual Harassment Crisis

What to do when things go wrong

If I hear of an employee losing the company money I'll be understanding. However, if I hear of any employee losing Salomon one shred of reputation I'll be ruthless.

—Warren Buffett
Testimony before the House Telecommunications
and Finance Subcommittee on the value
of corporate reputation

QUICK RESPONSE PAYS OUT IN PRICELESS REPUTATION MANAGEMENT

In 1997, CNA Financial Corp., a Chicago-based company with 19,000 employees, accepted the resignations of two of its top life insurance executives after harassment complaints were raised against one of them and reported to the other. The CEO was the accused, and the harassment was reported to the number two person in the company. According to the *Wall Street Journal* article announcing the investigation and the resulting resignations, the insurance company's announcement reflected an increased willingness of major corporations to deal quickly with such accusations. In this case, the company took swift action and addressed both policy violations head-on, with total disregard for the positions the executives held. CNA's quick response to investigating and acting upon the inappropriate behavior displayed by two of its most valuable company leaders showed that the company meant business when it said it had a zero tolerance for sexual harassment. Its tough stance paid off big in protecting the corporate reputation, something that many companies forget to factor in until irreparable damage is done.

In February, a month before the resignations, two female employees complained that Kettler, the president of CNA Life (a unit of CNA Financial), was making unwanted and offensive sexual remarks to them. They told the president's deputy, Teske, but had no response to their complaints. In a public statement the company announced the resignation of the president and his deputy, saying that Jack Kettler had made "offensive comments" and that Robert Teske had failed to act. Unlike most companies facing such a situation, CNA went even farther in taking its "stand-up" position. Proactively, instead of letting corporate attorneys and public relations consultants pull up the drawbridge, the company did the unusual and initiated communication with the media. Instead of ducking calls and issuing the typical "we vehemently deny any wrongdoing," the company contacted news organizations about the resignations and spoke with reporters. Although the company did not go into detail about the nature of the comments made or verified that in fact they were of a sexual nature, it was a big step for the company to reach out to the media about management's concern for the enforcement of company policy and the well-being of all the employees.

We do know that sexual harassment can and does occur in the best of companies. And despite a company's all-out efforts to reduce it, a few human beings occasionally act irresponsibly. CNA proved to many that as a company it knows how to act responsibly even when some of its employees, the highest-ranking employees in this case, do not.

THE CORE OF A CRISIS

We can inform and educate employees on what sexual harassment is, but we cannot make the personal decision for them when it comes to how they choose to behave. "Free will" does exist within corporate America, as long as it is understood that the choice to act irresponsibly has a price.

On the other hand, irresponsible behavior is not the exclusive province of employees. Sometimes the company is a greater offender than the harasser. A company's reaction or lack of response can often be as offensive and as destructive as the original act of harassment. Most employers and employees who have experienced a claim of sexual harassment gone sour inside a company—a claim that no one will take the responsibility for guiding through any internal order—will describe the experience as a nightmare. People turn against each other, walls go up, fighting positions are taken, and the essential elements of a business environment are replaced by primal combat tactics.

When I go into a workplace that has been victimized by the absence of rules of order and has recently experienced a badly managed sexual harassment crisis, the employees express feelings typical of any dysfunctional environment. There is anger, despair, bitterness, and distrust. Many are angry at the person who raised the complaint, some are angry at the accused, and almost all employees have some resentment toward management. One man told me it was as if they had a fire and they found out the hard way that the company had no working fire alarm, exits, or sprinkling system. At this particular company, people had banded into groups, and, interestingly, those people weren't clustered together based on hierarchy. The employees had drawn closer to others who shared the "same take" on what had happened to their company and who they believed was at fault. They had divided themselves according to similar "thinking." This company had a long way to go to resolve the longer-lasting damages of the sexual harassment claim that had hit the organization. Management had groaned about the cost of the settlement it had to pay two employees, but it wasn't until later that the company realized that the costs it was incurring for low morale, impacted performance, and broken-spirited employees were much higher than any one-time cash settlement.

THE FOUR STAGES OF A CRISIS

There are four stages of a crisis within an organization when a claim of sexual harassment occurs.

STAGE ONE: THE CULTURAL CLIMATE

The culture of a company—how it is run, the personalities of those running it, and the level of sexual activity already taking place—often determines if there is fertile ground for sexual harassment to occur; in other words, is there a preexisting hostile environment? In the case of Astra USA and Del Laboratories, the companies both had histories of an environment so hostile toward women that it had become part of their actual culture.

STAGE TWO: THE ACT OF HARASSMENT

This is the stage at which sexual harassment actually occurs within the workplace. This stage is the series of events, activities, and behaviors that is identified as the illegal action.

STAGE THREE: THE TRANSITION

The transition stage marks the time when a person feeling victimized strikes back. The person has reached the point where the behavior is intolerable. At this stage, an employee either reports the incidents to someone in the company or goes outside the company and files charges through a state division of human rights or through the Equal Employment Opportunity Commission.

STAGE FOUR: THE RESOLUTION

Resolution can come in many forms, but only a few of them are legal or healthy for all involved. One poor way to resolve a harassment situation takes this course: Someone is so tortured by sexual harassment at work that he or she can no longer endure the harassment and leaves the company. Legally this is called *constructive discharge.* This type of resolution is not good for anyone. It's bad for the victim because he or she is forced out of a job by illegal sexual behavior. It's bad for the company because the victim can sue and will likely be successful at it.

Another, unfortunate, way to resolve a complaint is to make the complainant feel like a pariah in the workplace. I hate to admit it, but even in 1999, companies are still committing the tactical error of making complainants feel like troublemakers instead of workers with a strong sense of decency.

The responsibility of resolution falls largely on the shoulders of the company, although those who feel they have been harassed or witnessed harassment have certain responsibilities as well. Cases of harassment should be reported promptly and truthfully, and individuals should be as cooperative as possible. Resolution only works if both employees and their employers take the process seriously.

WHAT COMPANIES SHOULDN'T DO

Some of the most common positions companies take when they are unsure of what to do with a claim of sexual harassment only add fuel to the fire. These positions are more telling about a company's real agenda regarding sexual harassment in the workplace than the company should admit:

Pretend that sexual harassment isn't a problem in the workplace or in any other place in corporate America.

Create a corporate culture that allows employees to think that their company is exempt from the rules.

Institute a policy, distribute it, and then have no idea how, or no intention, to carry it out.

Have untrained employees carry out investigations and conduct training.

Intimidate workers who report harassment.

Openly express displeasure at those who have reported harassment, sending a message to others that reporting harassment will hurt someone's career.

Overdiscipline employees without understanding the disciplinary process and making the punishment fit the crime.

DISCIPLINE GONE BAD

What can be as bad as not disciplining someone at all for serious and persistent sexual harassment? Perhaps it is overdisciplining an employee without understanding what the appropriate discipline is—as in making the punishment suit the crime. A couple of companies found out the hard way about the manner and extent of disciplining employees.

A SAD CASE OF DISCIPLINE

AT&T employee Holt Euliss was considered a good employee with a perfect record prior to getting hit with a claim of sexual harassment. In 1992, Euliss, an engineer in the corporation's North Carolina office, told Angela Rhew, a clerk who worked on the same floor that he did, an off-color joke. The joke was an old one, about a tailor who outlines the pockets on the bodice of a woman's dress with white chalk marks. When the woman tells the tailor that she wanted the pockets on the hips, the tailor brushes the chalk off the bodice and touches the woman's breasts while doing so. When Euliss told Angela Rhew the joke, he also acted out what the tailor had done in the joke.

According to news articles, Rhew also may have shared the joke with a few other secretaries, and some said that it was no big deal. But Rhew did tell her boss, who reported it immediately to the sexual harassment officer. Euliss admitted he had told the joke but said he only touched Angela's "upper torso." Euliss was escorted off company grounds, was asked to hand over his AT&T identification, and was told not to return to work until the company notified him.

It was reported that most employees viewed Euliss as a very shy man. According to employees who worked with both of them, Euliss had known Rhew for a great number of years and, as they were both divorced, did odd jobs around the house for her as well as help her out with her son's Little League team. When interviewed by the investigator handling the internal claim for AT&T, Rhew revealed that Euliss had told her offensive jokes before and had hinted that she may owe him something for all the help he gave her and her son. She had never complained about him before. It is not clear from sources whether Euliss was only chiding Rhew for taking advantage of his good nature or not.

As a result of the investigation, Euliss received a 30-day suspension without pay, a reduction in benefits, and a transfer to projects thousands of miles away from North Carolina. When he was notified of AT&T's decision to send him to worksites that would take him away from his daughter (he had joint custody with his ex-wife), he shot himself at his home.

AT&T is known to have a very good program on sexual harassment and seems to work hard at educating its employees. I don't know what exactly happened during this investigation, nor do I know the employees involved. I do know that this is a very tragic story and that there are many more true stories about sexual harassment that end like this. A number of deaths have been reported as a result of sexual harassment claims. The most important lesson to be taken from this sad story is that sexual harassment claims are a huge responsibility for anyone who is involved in both responding to and resolving them.

OTHER FORMS OF VIOLENCE

Workplace violence is a very real concern for companies today, and sometimes cases of sexual harassment become scenes of workplace violence in an instant, particularly when a situation is not handled properly. Here's what might occur if companies are not careful:

- When an employee is being harassed and a company has not stepped in to stop the harassment, the perpetrator can continue to "stalk" the complainant and endanger his or her life. Workplace stalking has become more common and the methods of stalking have increased with the advancements in communication and technology. Employees have killed other employees when they have been rebuffed. Because companies do not really know how far a harasser will go to get the attention of another employee, it can never be assumed that a situation will not reach a tragic end.

- Employees fired for sexual harassment have returned to the workplace and killed the complainants, witnesses, human resource people, management, or innocent people who happened to be in their line of fire. Companies must take great care in the manner in which they investigate and then terminate an employee in serious cases of sexual harassment. Legal counsel should always be consulted, and a well-planned termination procedure should include the assistance of company security.

- Those fired for sexual harassment also have been known to sabotage companies and harass, in other ways, the victim or witnesses. Companies must be in close contact with those who have experienced harassment after the harasser has left the company to make sure they are not experiencing any kind of off-site harassment.

IF YOU NEED TO REPORT SEXUAL MISCONDUCT OR SEXUAL HARASSMENT

The thought of reporting any kind of misconduct to the management of an organization makes the heart of any working man or woman beat quickly, not to mention that it makes the heart of an organization skip a beat when it receives such a report. It is frightening to step forward to speak about someone else's conduct, particularly if it is sexual. What the EEOC has been asking companies to do in the past several years is to create fair environments, establish procedures, and properly train those receiving complaints so that employees aren't so concerned about their own well-being that they are too afraid to speak up about something that the company legally and morally needs to know about.

Whether to report sexual misconduct or the existence of a social-sexual relationship that is interfering with work is a difficult but necessary decision. If you conduct yourself in a professional manner and understand how the process works, your task will be easier and your load of responsibility lighter. If you communicate clearly, you can reduce and even eliminate any suspicion that you might be saying something that would purposely bring you personal gain or that would unfairly attack and malign another employee.

HOW TO STEP FORWARD

There is a time, there should be a place, and there is definitely a way in which to report sexual harassment and sexual misconduct.

BEFORE YOU REPORT

Do a quiet but thorough check beforehand and make sure you are going to the appropriate place to report it. Most companies have established grievance procedures—if you haven't been informed of what they are through training or detailed descriptions in your employee handbook, look closely at your company policy. The policy should spell out your options for reporting. If your direct supervisor is the one who is offending you, then obviously you cannot report the behavior to that individual. Usually companies will offer several options for reporting inappropriate behavior, for example, taking your claim to the president's office or reporting it to human resources. If you are at a small company, take your complaint directly to the top person. That person cares the most about the business and will be the one most interested in resolving your concern.

Reflect upon what happened and the reason you need to report someone else's behavior. Based upon what you know about sexual harassment and sexual misconduct, is there validity to what you are saying? Reporting inappropriate behavior isn't about whether you like someone or not. Make sure you don't have any hidden, unacknowledged "other" reasons for reporting this person other than your named and identified concern. This is the time to be very honest with yourself, not *after* you have made a claim. Reporting another person's behavior is a serious action and one that should be done for no other reason than for you to behave responsibly when someone else has not.

TIMING

If you need to report sexual harassment, make an appointment, even if it is only for later in the same day. Making an appointment sets the tone by making it official business. An appointment alerts the person receiving your complaint that you have a matter of importance to discuss. Setting aside a specific time allows the other person to give your concern the proper attention. Also to your advantage, by having a time set aside, you know that you will be able to have an uninterrupted talk, making what can be a difficult task less daunting.

It is *not* to your advantage to just drop in on the person you intend to complain to, or to call this person on a cell phone while the person is in traffic or trying to catch a plane. Also, if you show up unexpectedly, the person may decide that you are impulsive and may not take you seriously.

And the most important point regarding timing is to report sexual harassment as soon as possible. Those who delay reporting harassment for months, even years, most always deal with the issue of credibility. Why did someone wait? By reporting sexual misconduct in a timely fashion, you give your company every opportunity to address and resolve it properly.

THE PLACE

Arrange for the meeting to take place in a quiet office or area where you feel comfortable talking openly. Be sure the setting is as professional as possible. *Don't* talk to someone in authority about this issue while meeting over a drink in a bar, having lunch, in passing in the hallway, while seated next to the person at a company function, while in the rest room, or while you are working on a project with a tight deadline. The reporting should take place when the management representative is prepared to discuss only your problem. Mentioning it in any other less suitable setting will diminish your intentions and may look like something other than the official report it needs to be.

HOW TO SAY IT

Before you go into the meeting, decide what your are going to say. This is no time to be vague or to use expressions that imply indecisiveness about what occurred or what was said. "He *sort* of touched my leg." If someone put his hand on your knee, say it. Describe where you were, what you were doing at the time, what was being said, and what happened before and after. This is all part of recounting the circumstances of the harassment.

It should go something like this:

> THE OPENING: I appreciate your taking the time to talk to me about a serious problem I am experiencing here at work. I have come to talk to you today because I understand that you are the person I am supposed to report these matters to. I am having a problem with Jack, and his behavior toward me is interfering with my ability to perform my job.

> THE FACTS: Last week, while just the two of us were working late on the Alpha World project, Jack said . . . or did . . . this to me. I responded by telling him to leave me alone or I would report

him. This is the second time he has made such a remark (and/or advance) to me. Previously it happened two weeks ago. At that time, I told him never to say (and/or do) that to me again. I thought it would stop, but as of last week, it has not.

THE PERSONAL FACTOR: Ms. Dowling, I was shocked and deeply offended by Jack's actions. This type of behavior is offensive to me and makes it very difficult for me to do my job under these circumstances.

CORPORATE LOYALTY AND REINFORCEMENT: As you know, I take my job and my position with this company very seriously. I normally enjoy my work and have found this to be a great place to work. I came to you today because I knew that I could talk to you about this, and I knew that you would understand. I wanted to do the right thing.

ASK FOR HELP: I am asking you and the company to help me solve this problem. I don't believe that I can handle it by myself. My attempts to get Jack to stop haven't been successful. I need your help in correcting Jack's behavior and preventing it from happening again.

In your effort to ask the company and the person you made the report to for help, include the following points in your discussion:

- Bring forth any physical items that may be pertinent to your decision (notes, copies of e-mails, or a chronological time line if there was more than one instance of inappropriate behavior).
- Reconfirm that the person you made your report to is the right person to discuss this type of grievance with at your company.
- If the behavior you are reporting is sexual, make it clear to the interviewer that you are very clear on the legal definition of what harassment is and it *was* sexual harassment that you experienced.
- Be definite about the kind of help you are seeking. Help the company help you.

- Let your employer know that you are amenable to working things out. It is not the company you are upset with, it is the individual(s) behaving inappropriately that has you concerned.

- Let your employer know that you found the behavior serious enough that you felt the need to document it, and kept a journal of times, dates, and the nature of the incidents.

- If it's not offered, set up a follow-up meeting.

- Document your discussion.

If you have any concern that the manager you are reporting the incidents to might join forces with the manager (or coworker) you are reporting, send a written and confidential follow-up letter (keep a copy) that basically reiterates your concern and your need for help. This legitimizes your report. Keep the tone of your letter positive, and thank the person for his or her time and concern.

WHEN A MANAGER RECEIVES A REPORT

- As a manager, take all reports of sexual harassment and sexual misconduct seriously, because they are serious. Regardless of the manner in which you receive the report, it is still the report of sexual harassment that needs to be addressed.

- If an employee requests that you don't act upon a claim, but just listen to his or her concern, let the employee know that legally you aren't permitted to do that. You cannot address an issue of possible harassment without having the company look into it.

- Don't ignore someone's report because you personally don't find the described behavior offensive. It's not your claim. Also, don't dismiss someone's report because you don't think much of that person or value the person's work. And don't think for one minute that if you ignore someone's report, the person will just go away. If someone reports sexual misconduct, you can be certain that he or she will be back to see what you've done to help. If the person doesn't inquire about the status of the investigation, then you will probably hear from the legal counsel the person has hired during the time you sat on the investigation.

- Don't give fatherly, or motherly, or brotherly, or old pal advice to someone with a professional concern regarding his or her well-being in the place of work. A professional worker is making a report of illegal behavior. Respond like a professional.

- If you are not in a human resources position but have received a report because you are the supervisor of the person complaining, take the complaint to the proper person immediately. If your company's policy dictates that all internal investigations are conducted through specific channels, *do not try to investigate a claim on your own.*

Some supervisors have made the mistake of trying to contain a complaint by "keeping it in the family" of the department where it originated. Several errors occur when a complaint is handled this way. Usually managers have no experience in investigating claims of sexual harassment. They don't know what to look for, and they don't understand the manner in which claims are substantiated. The issue of confidentiality is also key to protecting both the process of investigation and the involved parties. I have seen supervisors think that they have "handled" a complaint only to have the complainants bring up a grievance at a later date. Usually, when they bring another incident to the attention of someone in the company, they often go above the supervisor they brought their first claim to because this time they are more upset and looking for someone who can make the behavior stop. The company's liability for the first report not being handled properly is very high if the claim should find its way into formal legal proceedings.

Also, when supervisors attempt to investigate a claim, their own investigation may interfere with the formal investigation being conducted by the human resources department. Having two investigations going on at the same time creates confusion, contaminates the fact-finding process, and disturbs employees and adversely affects their productivity.

- Do not treat the person who brings forth a complaint differently. Complainants are extremely sensitive about retaliation. It is the second biggest fear regarding sexual harassment. They are afraid that after they report sexual harassment, they will be shunned by both those they reported it to and those they reported.

Remember: The majority of people who report sexual harassment aren't interested in causing trouble. They are interested in ending it. The reason for the report is usually because someone else's behavior is so troubling, or frightening, or offensive, that the complainants have nowhere else to turn except to the company they work for. They are coming for help. True, sometimes people report sexual harassment for the wrong reasons. False claims do occur. But skilled investigators can usually flush out a trumped-up claim by knowing where to look for the subtle inconsistencies in stories and actual events.

STEPPING UP TO
SEXUAL HARASSMENT COMPLAINTS

Data from the Institute for Crisis Management indicates that "sexual harassment continues to be the fastest-growing crisis in the 1990s, with its media coverage up 276 percent from 1990," *PR News* reported. So the chances that the media will cover an employee's sexual harassment complaint (especially one that is not handled properly by a company) are extremely high. How a company handles news of a claim, both internally and externally, during critical early moments can have a lasting impact on a company's image, morale—and, certainly, profits.

For a company that finds itself thrown into a front-page story about sexual harassment, addressing complaints inside the company can be overwhelming when the press is already on the phone looking for answers. Here are a few guidelines to keep in mind:

Develop a strategy that addresses the problem. When dealing with the media, remember that you are representing the entire company. Refrain from trying your case in the press. It shows no sensitivity toward your employees, and it won't win you or your company any public approval.

Have one spokesperson. Have only one person speak for your company. If there is more than one spokesperson, the message may not be consistent, and it may reveal confusion and disorder within. It's best that the person chosen be your top person or a well-trained company spokesperson. It should never be a consultant.

Know your stuff. This is where having solid sexual harassment policies, programs, and procedures is key. Know them cold and be able to talk about them. The media are generally suspicious (and rightfully so) of managers who stumble over the name of their human resources manager or can't speak intelligently about their company's commitment to a workplace free of sexual harassment.

WHAT TO SAY

Ideally, a company spokesperson should have media training *before* the company is involved in a crisis. Many mid-size to large companies put their top management and company spokespersons through media training to help them learn the proper ways to answer questions from all types of audiences, especially the press, *before a crisis erupts.* Here are some more guidelines to keep in mind:

Sound like a good employer. Protect the rights of your employees in all statements you make internally and to the media.

Understand the media's interest. Be fair, honest, and direct with reporters. Respond to their requests to the fullest possible extent, even though you can't, of course, give them confidential information.

Have a crisis team, but keep it small. Your team should consist of those who can advise and inform you on all aspects of media inquiries, legal actions, and internal processes, but it should be oriented toward results.

Communicate with your employees. As important as public statements are, when faced with a crisis, managers must never forget that their employees are their most important audience and their best representatives. If your company is going to be making headlines, let the employees know, in a general way, what is going on. Don't let them learn about what you and other top managers are thinking by reading it in the newspaper. Properly addressing claims of sexual harassment within a company is as much about understanding human nature as it is about understanding the legal issues that surround it.

Corporate Comebacks

Moving On When There Is No Going Back

CHAPTER 11

The Costs of Corporate Sex, Sexual Misconduct, and Sexual Harassment

To extraordinary circumstances we must apply extraordinary remedies.

—Napoleon Bonaparte

ONE SIDE

"When I ended up in a lawsuit with my former employer, I couldn't believe how fast I went from being financially secure to being on the edge of bankruptcy. I hadn't gotten more than two weeks severance. While the case proceeded, I had trouble getting a job. My attorney, although on a contingency agreement, wanted me to pay for court fees and expert witnesses' time, and before I knew it, I had over $25,000 in legal fees in front of me, with no court date. I let my health insurance lapse, couldn't make my house or car payments, and couldn't afford to keep up with what it was costing me to "network" while looking for a new job. I was so tired from what I had been through during the period of time my boss was harassing me, by the time he fired me, I didn't think I had the strength to go on, to get past everything. I felt like someone was shooting at me everyday, and often hit me. My personal relationships suffered so much that I can't really talk about it. I know that I am having trouble trusting people, certainly men. I hope I will be able to go to work for someone again, someday, but I just don't know. I've lost my passion for work, I guess. Within a year, I had been sexually harassed, lost my job, my health insurance, and my credit rating, and was faced with great debt and a long climb back to where I was, careerwise. I won $113,000, in the end. How much did it all cost me? In my heart, it cost me everything I was, everything I had, and everything I hoped to be someday. You tell me how you can convert that into money. You can't. No one can."

Margie, age 28
Employee

THE OTHER

"When I got word that one of our managers in Oklahoma was accused of harassment, I had to get involved with human resources people and lawyers, and put aside my own calendar, which was already overloaded with commitments. It was incredible the amount of time that I personally had to put into dealing with this claim. At first, I did feel bad for Shawna. I think something happened to her, but something pretty damaging happened to my company, too. I have worked very, very hard to build this company into one that is now profitable enough to sue. Shawna was never a good worker. I know that for a fact, because I spend a great deal of time in that office. Now, because of something Frank said, she wants $500,000 of my profits. The suit was filed in February. We are only four months into it, and I have made eight trips to Oklahoma, and have a total of four attorneys and two human resources people working on it almost full-time. My legal fees are averaging five figures a month. Our public relations agency has added to our needs a crisis plan with a $200,000 budget attached to it. I'm in for a million dollars, at the very least, and Shawna's at her desk, figuring out on her calculator how much she can keep after taxes. The other employees are split on how they feel about her, Frank can't manage her anymore, so she's free to do whatever she wants. Other employees resent that she's not doing her share of the work. We haven't had decent numbers come out of that office since the claim was filed. I am just waiting to have someone from *Dateline* or *20/20* sitting out in the oil field ready to do a story on what a bad guy I am. This is not fair. I believe that the government is really putting an unfair burden on American businesses. My business is going to take a huge hit

---

SOME NUMBERS

In 1988, a study done by the U.S. Merit Systems Protection Board showed that sexual harassment over ten years ago cost the federal government $267.3 million.

In 1994, Baker and McKenzie, a law firm, was asked to pay $7.1 million in punitive damages to a former secretary.

In 1995, Wal-Mart Stores had a $50 million verdict for punitive damages reduced to $5 million for a victim of sexual harassment.

In 1997 $2 million was awarded to three female employees of a California prison.

In 1997 Astra USA was told to pay $10 million to women who had been sexually harassed at the company.

In 1998 Mitsubishi was asked to pay $34 million in addition to already paying almost $9 million in a private suit.

---

because of this case. I hope it survives it. I'm starting to wonder."

Joe, age 46
Business owner

SECRET SETTLEMENTS AND SETTLEMENT "SECRETS"

Coming up with actual bottom-line figures for how much sexual harassment is costing all of us these days would be nothing short of a good estimate. Most sexual harassment cases settle out of court, and therefore settlement figures are not publicly disclosed. Even

---

HOW MUCH IS SEXUAL HARASSMENT
REALLY COSTING US?*

A female lab technician complained to the EEOC that her employer promoted men more than women. The employer responded that she was not promoted because she engaged in improper conduct. As a result of the EEOC complaint, she got additional training but no promotion. She filed a suit against her employer.

Verdict: $4,200,000

A female employee at a tobacco processing plant claimed that she was sexually harassed by employees she supervised. After she complained to management, the employees retaliated by slowing down production. Management offered her a transfer but took no action against the others. The hostile work environment led to her resignation. Her lawsuit alleged "constructive discharge."

Verdict: $2,000,000

*Source: Monitor Liability Managers, Inc. (A member company of W. R. Berkley Corporation)

---

when companies settle cases internally, settlement costs appear in a different cost category than one might think. Settlement figures may be posted as severance or another cost of doing business such as a downsizing need.

According to the *Washington Post*, "Because of these secrecy agreements, there is no way to measure how many cases of sexual harassment involving CEOs or other high-level corporate officials are settled quietly. But experts said the number of such cases is higher than anyone would suspect." I agree. A great deal of money is being spent in corporate America that we aren't being told about, and for good reason. First, if a settlement is reached privately, out of court, technically it isn't the public's business what the final figure might be. To many companies, *that is the incentive for settlements.* They are private resolutions to a conflict situation, and they are usually designed to remain confidential. Most companies do not want to admit they are paying out anything for sexual harassment complaints. Payoffs are something companies don't want their employees to know about for fear there will be a soup line of employees standing outside the human resources director's office.

Unfortunately, not all employees who threaten to sue their employers actually have serious claims. Sometimes claims seem frivolous, and perhaps financially driven, and companies need to protect themselves from those employees who are aware of the nuisance-factor incentive. As the number of cases of sexual harassment has increased, so has the number of plaintiff attorneys practicing in this area, and so has the number of claims that don't meet the legal standards of what sexual harassment is in today's workplace.

Back in 1988, well over ten years ago, *Working Woman* magazine and Klein and Associates released a study on what sexual harassment was costing Fortune 500 companies. This study calculated that sexual harassment costs the typical Fortune 500 company $6.7 million per year in absenteeism, turnover, low morale, and lost productivity. By 1997, according to *CFO* magazine, companies may now be spending around $1 billion to settle sexual harassment cases. Attorneys estimate that the average cost to settle a claim at the very, very early stages is approximately $10,000 to $15,000. In my work, it has been a few years since most of the settlements I have witnessed have been anything under $50,000. In fact, in the past several years, I have seen companies spend millions of dollars defending themselves and paying out settlements. I believe that corporate America would be shocked if it knew the amount companies are paying out yearly for sexual harassment disturbances.

The settlement price has gone up with each court decision since the Civil Rights Act of 1991 went into play and offered plaintiffs the opportunity to sue for both compensatory and punitive damages. Monetary relief for victims of sexual harassment increased from $7 million in 1991 to $49 million in 1997, according to government figures tracking public settlements. And there's no reason to think the upward trend has not continued.

INSURING THE COMPANY— ASSURING THE BOARD

More and more companies are protecting themselves by taking out insurance policies that will pay some of the costs of these suits. Insurance companies like Monitor Liability Managers, Inc., Chubb, American International Group, and Reliance National offer policies called employment practices liability insurance to protect employers from a range of employee claims, including sexual harassment. Policy premiums cost about $10,000 yearly for $1 million in coverage, with a minimum of a $5,000 deductible. Policies usually cover legal costs, front and back pay, and compensatory damages. What the policies don't cover is possible punitive awards, because in certain states companies are not allowed to insure themselves for employees' specific intentional acts.

HOW MUCH IS SEXUAL HARASSMENT AND MISCONDUCT COSTING INDIVIDUALS?

Individuals suffer greatly in sexual harassment disputes. Whether you are the accuser or the accused, the cost can include life-altering damages. When employees find they are being subjected to sexual harassment, here are some of the costs they experience for being a target:

LOSS OF ENTHUSIASM

Often victims of sexual harassment will start to lose their enthusiasm for their company, their job, and even their choice of career. Because of the amount of energy required to fend off the offender, often on a daily basis, an employee facing harassment will start to feel differently about going into work every day. In fact, more than 20 percent of women who are sexually harassed give up and quit their job.

Victims frequently become depressed and develop a sense of hopelessness. The victims will begin to feel that there is no way out. If they are concerned about reporting the behavior (because they don't trust their company's grievance channels or are afraid of retaliation from the perpetrator), they feel as though the next steps—reporting or leaving, and being forced to look for another job—are overwhelming. One woman told me she was so angry that she was put in such a position, the anger started to make her sick. Another told me that she "lost her will to fight." She said that she felt as though she had been beaten into a corner. Her self-esteem was gone, and she started to believe that she deserved to be going into a job where her boss was harassing her. She began to think of her contributions as worthless and her life meaningless. In her words, "He made me stop dreaming about my future. Suddenly I just hoped that I would get through the day."

CHANGES IN SOCIAL AND SEXUAL BEHAVIOR

Many men and women have told me that when they experienced sexual harassment in their workplaces, they lost interest in socializing with people they worked with and even with their friends. They found they wanted to escape from their jobs and "hide away" in their homes. They often retreated into activities that didn't require them to interact with people—like watching television.

Many victims complain of problems in their personal relationships. Intimacy and sex become a problem. Some say the whole notion of sex turns them off since they are disgusted by their superiors' sexual advances. Others become very "clingy" with their spouses and become almost helpless and childlike in their marriages. One man said that his wife was always strong and independent. When she started "having trouble at work with her boss," she started to act like a "meek, almost subservient wife." He did not know how to help her find her way back to her old self because he was afraid to even talk to her about her changed behavior. He was concerned about saying anything that she might think was criticism. He knew she was on the edge of a breakdown and it wouldn't take much to push her over the edge.

Sometimes the spouse of the employee experiencing sexual harassment will be thrown into a turmoil. The spouse will feel a sense of helplessness and frustration because he or she can't immediately "fix" the harassment situation, at least, not without doing something that would have negative consequences. A sad case in point: One woman lost her job after her boss attempted to rape her in her office. Her husband became deeply disturbed over her misfortune. When the company began to drag her through the mud in the pretrial processes, he killed himself and left his wife to deal with even more problems.

SENSE OF ISOLATION

Some victims of sexual harassment feel there is no one else who can understand what they are going through. Despite the fact that they may have a loving family or supportive spouse, they still feel as though they are going through the harassment alone. Women will often say that even when they have a wonderful marriage or relationship with a man, they will start to notice gender differences and resent their husbands. One secretary felt that her husband was just giving her lip service when he tried to comfort her. At times, she said, she looked at him and thought how unfair it was that he was a man, and that the men in her life were always in charge, always controlling. She couldn't believe her own feelings, but she was actually resentful of the fact that her husband was a member of what she believed was the ruling class—men—just because one man, in particular, was now ruining her career.

INCREASED SENSE OF FEAR

One employee told me that she suddenly thought "everyone" was about to assault her. One evening, she was at the grocery store leaning over the frozen foods and caught someone's movement out of the corner of her eye. The man had a beige jacket on, much like her boss wore. She dropped her frozen vegetables and let out a small scream. Her own jumpiness made her realize that her nerves were shot. All day long, she worried about her boss pulling one of his surprise moves on her. She realized she couldn't shut it off when she left work.

HOW MUCH IS SEXUAL HARASSMENT COSTING COMPANIES AND THEIR EMPLOYEES?

Shirley Chisholm once said that when morality comes up against profit, it is seldom that profit loses. In the bigger picture on sexual harassment, on the surface that may seem to be the case. But at closer examination, the money a company thinks it is saving by not acknowledging a sexual harassment problem, it may be losing in other ways.

When employees work in an environment where they are subjected to anything that interferes with their ability to perform their jobs, it is going to affect many aspects of the company's business. When even one employee is affected by sexual harassment, every employee within that department will feel some negative effect. Distrust of management's ability to resolve an employee's problem can begin almost immediately. If employees feel that management is fumbling through the resolution process—or worse, turning against the employee with the complaint— other employees will instantly consider the "what if this were me" possibility.

Other times, employees will seem to turn against the complaining employee, and be angry with that person for "causing all this trouble." When companies are slow or clumsy in the way they handle a complaint, they allow their employees to become emotionally or even actively involved in the dispute. I have worked within companies where the dispute has already taken over a department. People aren't speaking to each other, or if they are, they are whispering to a selected few in the parking lot or rest room. Employees, without even realizing what is happening, will start to "review and evaluate" those named in the

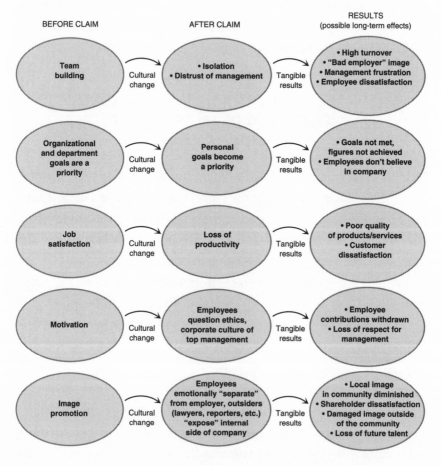

The effects of sexual harassment claims on the workplace.

dispute. For example, if it is a woman who has made the complaint against her male boss, employees might start talking about the woman's sex life, her marriage or dating life, the way she dresses, her motives, her financial situation, her ability to do her job—in fact, you name it, and people have discussed it.

Those accused face similar fates, regardless of the merit of the claim. Supervisors accused of harassment may find they have an unwanted "cheering section" of loyal employees who will openly support their boss and trash the complainant. On the other hand, the complaint gives some employees a reason to really dislike their hard-driving boss. Upper management will certainly treat an accused supervisor differently if the company doesn't know or understand why a claim was filed. All it knows is that it doesn't want any claims and this supervisor somehow made one "happen."

Some workplace friends will find themselves sharing secrets about a coworker who is involved in a sexual harassment dispute because they want to appear as if they are "insiders." When a company lets acts of sexual harassment or a claim of harassment go unchecked or unresolved, it will create such a great rift between employees that the damages frequently will be too great to ever be repaired. Once employees turn against one another, helping them rebuild their working relationships with one another is almost impossible.

HOW MUCH IS SEXUAL MISCONDUCT COSTING US AS A SOCIETY?

Sexual harassment is a crime against our own personal beliefs and the integrity of our working community. Even though the exact definition of sexual harassment may be unclear to some, serious sexual wrongdoing is something everyone seems to find damaging and offensive. Much like illegal conduct such as blackmail and extortion, serious sexual misconduct crosses an individual's tolerance lines—it becomes something sinister.

It is true that for many years the impact of sexual harassment in our society was something that mostly women and their special-interest groups understood. That has changed. Now, it is quite evident that both men and women realize this behavior is costing companies, individuals, and our society as a whole too much in terms of human lives, organizational energy, and money.

I believe that the really hard costs of sexual harassment to businesses is felt most in what it does to the heart of an organization. In terms of dollars and cents, much bigger than settlement costs is its impact on all employees within an organization and the changes it produces within a company.

According to a study conducted by Curtis Verschoor, a professor at DePaul University, companies committed to ethical business practices do better financially and have significantly greater representation among the top 100 financial performers than companies that don't. In fact, Verschoor found that companies committed to ethics are listed among the top 100 twice as often as those without an ethics focus. Just as important as having an ethical position, a company must have an internal program to enforce that position. Technically, ethics aren't viewed in the business community as being connected to strict accountability in sexual harassment, but they are certainly closely related. It appears that companies that have a strong business ethic apply that same ethic to protecting their employees from sexual discrimination.

CHAPTER 12

Keeping Good Company

Workplaces that work for everyone

Regarding ethics in the workplace in the twenty-first century:

When the onus is on the individual, individuals will reach decisions based on the same ethical standards they live by. As individual responsibility increases in business and in politics, a universal code of conduct will evolve; we will all hold ourselves and each other to higher standards of behavior.

—John Naisbitt
Global Paradox: The Bigger the World Economy,
the More Powerful Its Smallest Players
(Morrow, New York, 1994)

MEETING THE CHALLENGE

There is little question that there is work to do when it comes to creating working environments that can simultaneously meet business goals and meet all the needs of today's workers. Companies that can claim "we care, we're fair, and we have substantially increased our market share" when it comes to describing their corporate mission integrating both business goals and employee relations practices have probably developed and implemented a well-crafted strategic plan. It doesn't happen by chance. It occurs because of choice, commitment, and design.

Up until now, most companies have not found a clear path to a working environment that can be considered a model workplace. The truth is, it takes a great deal of work to create and maintain an environment that is built on a clear understanding of mutual expectations, that abides by rules that are fully and adeptly enforced, and that inspires human beings to treat each other fairly. It also takes time for an organization to develop and carry out such a mission. Most of all, it requires constant motivation on the part of both individuals and the organization itself.

And the essential motivation, to simply want to do something because "it is the right thing," often gets put aside when goals like remaining competitive and staying profitable take precedent. After all, said one very disgruntled business owner, it is a business, not a nonprofit organization, that he is trying to run. He is "up to his ears" in "government interference" regarding the kinds of people he needs to hire, always feeling like he has to be a camp counselor overseeing the way employees interact. Furthermore, the tasks of setting up policies and procedures for all of this "sex harassment business" is an unfair burden. He complains that it feels the way product liability did in his product area during the 1980s, except now the ticking bombs are inside his factory rather than coming from outside consumer concerns. He does not think company management should be the moral police for workers who want to cheat on their spouses, have affairs, hit on each other, or have social events that wouldn't necessarily appeal to everyone. It is personal choice and personal business, he said, and not something companies should be named in as an involved party.

So although the law is firmly in place regarding this issue, some companies, like the one noted above, are still balking at having to comply, and are showing strong reluctance in supporting the issue inside their own companies. These particular companies tell human resources to do the absolute minimum in this area. Don't overexpose the policy; just make sure it is somewhere in the handbook, they are told. And don't, for God's sake, encourage anyone to report anything. In these situations, and there are hundreds of thousands of companies doing business just like this, there is no such thing as motivation or the integration of new thinking. It's old thinking with a renewal sticker stuck on it saying the company vehicle has squeaked past discriminatory inspection for another year.

This kind of leadership attitude sprinkled throughout the business community has kept companies from tapping into their own resources and inventiveness to create workplaces that could really become models for those similar in design and size. Companies like these are not going to be motivated by the "do right because it is right" concept. Ultimately, they are going to be motivated by something more tangible: money. When lawsuits or internal disruptions cause enough of a stir and cost a company enough time, energy, and money, the company will address the issue of sexual misconduct in a manner that is not about protecting employees but is about protecting business. With money as the motivating factor, company leaders are addressing the concern, and perhaps along the way, they might recognize the long-term benefits of what they are doing for their most valuable asset in the whole mix—people.

GOOD PEOPLE MAKE GOOD COMPANIES

Companies must not underestimate the people who work for them. Employees today are different than they were even a decade ago, and companies must learn more about them. Nowadays, employees think differently from the employees of the seventies and the eighties, and their expectations of themselves and the companies they work for are also very different. Today's employees want more, and not necessarily just more power and money. Employees today value their *total lives* and their lives are defined by more than just the jobs they hold. They want to have more control over their own destiny. Once it was enough to say that a man or woman had a "good job." Now employees are changing the standard definition of what a good job means to each of them personally. A good job may mean that they have a strong sense of fulfillment from what they are doing, that they like the people they work for—and with—and, that their jobs allow them time to spend (without guilt) with their families. A good job may mean a good balance in life, allowing time to develop collegial working relationships and friendships and interests outside of work. Employees are not willing to sacrifice the loss of their self-esteem just to say that they work for an industry giant or a powerful network if they, in fact, work for a tyrant or a mean-spirited person and put in twelve-hour workdays. Working environments, including all the emotional, ethical, and spiritual parts of a workplace, matter to people.

When interviewing individuals who stood up and complained of sexual harassment, I found that there were two main forces that made them decide to speak up. First, there was the private pain of what they were being subjected to—and how it was affecting them on a deeply personal level. Second, it was their outrage at someone taking advantage of them in their own workplace to advance an agenda of illegal behavior. They felt challenged on a moral level. It was a duel of good versus evil, and they weren't going to submit to evil. These feelings weren't from one gender, either. Both men and women felt strongly about it. All of them were interested in protecting the integrity of their own workplaces, and if they had to take a personal hit in the process, it was worth it for their own sense of self.

CORPORATE ETHICS

The bigger concept of corporate ethics—companies doing the right thing—is truly at the heart of taking on the challenge and responsibility of reducing sexual misconduct in the workplace. The often unspoken question that many business leaders and even employees have about all of this is why should they embrace this challenge? Does it truly have any real benefits for the bottom line and the overall success of a business? How can it be done without taking away from the primary focus a company must have? These are fair questions, and at least the first question has been getting answered in some surprising ways.

Dr. Lottie Bailyn, professor of management at the Massachusetts Institute of Technology, was part of an expert team that did research for a project funded by the Ford Foundation called Relinking Work and Life. Dr. Bailyn and the team studied Xerox Corp., Corning Inc., and Tandem Computers from 1991 to 1995. According to the study, paying attention to employees' personal lives increases corporate productivity. The study indicated that old thinking that implied that workers should separate their personal lives (and problems) from work is an unrealistic concept in today's working world. The chief executive of Xerox, Paul Allaire, noted, "At a time when corporate America is being assailed for putting profits above all else, this study establishes that the best business strategy recognizes that greater employee satisfaction means greater productivity, and in turn, better business results."

Although the purpose of the fact-finding study was not about ethics per se, it did show that extraordinary results were achieved because management showed that it cared about workers. When management gave individuals the chance to control their own lives, and gave them the opportunity to be accountable for their own behavior, they took control and were accountable. Absenteeism dropped, creativity rose, quality and customer satisfaction improved, and projects were done under budget. As a director of human resources said, "All of this was due largely to creating an environment in which people were inspired to do their best." Being free from sexual harassment or unwanted sexual advances is certainly a key aspect of controlling one's own work environment.

CORPORATE REPUTATIONS ARE BOTTOM LINES AND TOP PRIORITY

According to Hiroshi Wald, a California-based research consultant, corporate reputation is built from the sum of a number of internal practices and can be destroyed by those same practices. A few years ago, when Smith Barney was accused of having a hostile work environment for women, it was proclaimed the "Merchant of Shame" by the National Organization for Women. It wasn't because the company's products were bad. It was because a special-interest group thought the company treated certain employees unfairly. Press releases flew out from NOW, and landed on the Internet, in the media, and squarely in front of the consumer. Corporate reputations are priceless. According to the 1998 Foundation for the School of Business at Indiana University, a corporate reputation is highly valued for a number of reasons. "It is easier to attract and keep talented people. Customers are more willing to purchase the firm's existing products and services and accept new offerings from it. Raising capital and borrowing funds are easier if investors and bankers perceive the firm favorably."

There are those who will argue that corporate ethics is not directly connected to the way a company responds to the issue of sexual harassment and sexual misconduct. I disagree. It is broadly understood that corporate ethics is about being committed both to the community and to the corporation's employees. I believe that allowing illegal sexual behavior to take place in a workplace is as serious as allowing any other unethical practice—financial, environmental, social, or otherwise—to knowingly occur. According to analysts and financial publications, shareholders are looking to companies to be responsible employers. How companies treat employees does matter, both on a short-term and long-term basis.

WHAT IS A MODEL WORKPLACE, AND WHERE CAN WE GET ONE?

The term *model workplace* began to bother me when it became the interchangeable buzzword for the moving-forward plan that Mitsubishi was hoping to achieve and the form of crisis management they were using. To say that a company in such turmoil was going to achieve a model workplace environment in a matter of a year was not realistic. What is and what is not a model workplace should be based upon the individual goals of a particular company and take into consideration the uniqueness of the organization's culture, the employees, and the nature of the business. There are certainly basic standards that all organizations can strive toward, but the methods and means of getting there may, and, in fact, should, be different. A model workplace for a company the size of Microsoft will surely not serve as an appropriate model for a small or start-up company.

I believe that each company must develop and reach its own level of a model workplace. A company's strengths and weaknesses should be considered when it comes to addressing sexual harassment and sexual misconduct, for companies, and the individuals who work for them, have different ways of responding to change. Truly addressing sexual harassment as it needs to be addressed requires most companies to introduce a new way of thinking and a different way of communicating on an interpersonal level. Companies should determine what methods of introducing these communication concepts would make their employees most receptive and responsive.

BUILD TO SUIT: THE RIGHT COMMUNICATION PROGRAM FOR YOUR COMPANY

SMALL COMPANIES: *THE PERSONALITY-DRIVEN ENVIRONMENT*

Organizations that are small or entrepreneurial, and whether a start-up or one that is long established but with few employees, need to develop and implement communication channels that suit both their structure and culture. Small companies often differ in their overall organizational needs from large corporations but not in their employees' needs. Sometimes the management of smaller organizations may feel that their best approach to all internal issues is to apply an overall policy that all who work for the company are "friends," part of a team, and need to always put the goals of the team first. That approach to managing people without any real organizational structure can be effective, for a while, when it comes to reaching business goals, but it falters when there is an internal crisis like sexual harassment. Individual employees, even those who seek out employment at loosely structured companies, still want their rights protected when they find them in danger of being violated. Small company environments that are built around dynamic leadership are perhaps one of the most desirable companies to work for, providing management uses their leadership to address important employment issues with the same enthusiasm and commitment they have to external goals of the company.

I recommend that small companies incorporate diversity, discrimination, and sensitivity education into their various professional development meetings and programs for their employees. I have found that high-energy, fast-growing companies that include these elements in yearly meetings while discussing new-products announcements, marketing strategies, and company growth, meet with very receptive employees. Often small companies will tap outside experts to present to their employees the latest information about these issues. Employees accept such information and education as part of their own professional growth and feel that it provides them tools to be better current or future managers of people.

I will do a presentation for a company only if the CEO is willing to participate in some way in the presentation. Most of them do want to participate and recognize how critical their visible commitment is to enforcing their policy from the top down. When the CEO of a company speaks openly about the importance of such issues during business meetings, the employees instantly understand and respect the company's position regarding zero tolerance of sexual harassment and sexual misconduct. They know it is serious business and because it is the president of their company speaking, they know the company takes it seriously.

Mid-size companies just beginning a program may face a greater challenge when it comes to bringing all employees together to discuss and learn about their company's policy and procedures regarding sexual harassment and discrimination. When I have been asked to educate a workforce of over a thousand employees, I base the roll-out of the program on the type of business, its locations, number of employees, and its organization structure and culture. When the employees realize that time and effort has been spent in creating thoughtful presentations to reach out to them, they are much more receptive to the company's policy. But most important is that well-developed customized programs will be the first important step toward developing a sense of trust between employer and employees. Employees will be likely to believe that their company will know how to proceed quickly and fairly if there is ever a need to bring forth a grievance. In turn, the management of the company will have a sense that employees understand their own responsibilities in creating an environment that meets the legal standards and the company's own standards.

BIG BUSINESS:
BIG OPPORTUNITIES FOR INNOVATION

When it comes to communicating and educating employees, the advantage of being a huge organization is obviously *resources*. Because large corporations are already able to communicate globally with customers and audiences, they already have the right thinking and mechanisms to communicate to any marketplace in the world, including their most

---

THE BASICS FOR ALL COMPANIES

- **Have a written policy.**   This should be clear and easy to understand and spell out what harassment is and that the company will not tolerate it. The language used should be from the EEOC's definition of sexual harassment. Consult with your company's attorney when drafting your policy. Make sure every single employee has a copy of it and read it.
- **Develop a grievance procedure.**   If an employee needs to complain, he or she needs to know where they need to report it. The persons receiving complaints should know how to receive complaints; and they, or someone else within the company, should know how to investigate and resolve them. (Again, consult with your company's attorney when setting up a grievance and investigative procedure.)
- **Educate, educate, and educate employees and management.** Policies and procedure won't matter if employees and management don't understand the importance of the issues and the laws they uphold. Don't overlook educating new employees, especially new managers, as they join the company.

---

important one: their employee population. For those with ample resources, technology is certainly one of the most innovative ways to reach out to employees. I believe that training and learning aids in corporate America within the next five years are going to be the most innovative and creative steps ever taken within the business community. On-line and interactive training will link education and employees that previously couldn't be reached. Building and sharing information and knowledge bases will help bridge the problems that both employees and employers have had over the past decade in figuring out just what best practice actually means and what a model workplace could and should look like.

Making the treatment of employees a top priority is the essence of successful business practices. Once both management and employees share a common understanding that having a policy and upholding it isn't about restricting behavior but improving it, dramatic change will occur. Whether a company has five employees or 50,000, if management is sincerely interested in educating their employees, they can, together, create a program that isn't separate from business goals, but is, in fact, an important part of them.

WHAT CAN BE DONE ABOUT THE PROBLEM OF SEXUAL BEHAVIOR IN THE WORKPLACE?

ONE: TAKE THE LEAD

Smart executives and managers at successfully run companies know that sexual misconduct cannot be tolerated in the workplace. Then why do some very powerful companies, in practice, look the other way when misbehavior occurs at the highest levels?

The public's generally disinterested reaction to President Clinton's behavior with a White House employee signaled that many Americans (and most people around the world) don't really care how the leader of their country behaves sexually. "Whatever he does in private is okay, as long as he is doing a good job leading the country," was the predominant attitude in the polls. In my work with corporations, I hear that same attitude from employees when they talk about their corporate leaders. As the general public did with Clinton, many can separate poor judgment in sexual matters from the way a person undertakes his or her job responsibilities. Most people would rather concentrate on the professional efficacy of their business leaders. Being a good leader—that's all that matters. Or is it?

I have worked with powerful executives at many different kinds of companies, and I have found that the most effective leaders believe that their professional responsibilities extend to all aspects of their personality. When a leader cannot refrain from personally breaking the rules that he or she is supposed to enforce professionally, it becomes very difficult to enforce any rules throughout the company. It is extremely shortsighted to allow the highest-ranking employees to abuse the rules. Eventually the employees get the signal that anything goes.

TWO: AGREE ON TERMS

In order for us to be able to understand what we can and cannot tolerate in the workplace, we need to agree on a definition of sexual harassment. We need a better understanding of what is expected of us at work both under the law and according to our individual companies' standards.

Some will argue that specifically defining sexual harassment will open the door for employees to file more law suits whenever they encounter even the hint of sexual innuendo at work. But in my own experience I have found that employees actually become more tolerant of other individuals' actions when those employees know that their company will act seriously and swiftly when and if a serious incidence of sexual harassment occurs. When employees have confidence in their company's ability to deal with harassment issues, that their grievance would be met without retaliation, they are less likely to overreact to the occasional sexual *faux pas.*

CASE STUDY—E.I. DUPONT DE NEMOURS AND COMPANY: PERSONAL SAFETY PROGRAM; A MATTER OF RESPECT*

E.I. DuPont de Nemours and Company is a diversified chemical, energy and specialty products company that has been in existence for over 180 years. Headquartered in Wilmington, Delaware, the company has approximately 114,000 employees.

DuPont's approach exemplifies how one company has successfully implemented the training component of diversity, without which any initiative would be insufficient. DuPont developed the Personal Safety Program to help employees address social issues such as sexual harassment, physical assault, spouse battering, child and elder abuse, and, particularly, how to confront rape in a responsible and meaningful way. In addition to providing rape prevention workshops for female employees as well as wives and adult female dependents of its employees, the company has established workshops for managers to help define their role in helping employees who are victims of rape either on or off the job. Corporate guidelines and services have been established to support the employee in the aftermath of rape. And finally, company-wide Personal Safety Meetings are held for all employees.

Out of this program emerged a workshop called "A Matter of Respect," which helps people find out where they can find support in the company. The workshop was created to help establish a responsible and respectful environment free of sexual harassment and discrimination. At the same time, it provides a means for acknowledgement and recognition of stereotypes. The four-hour workshop, which has been attended by approximately 80,000 of DuPont's employees, was launched in 1988. The workshop focuses on treating each other with respect, rather than on legal issues.

The program has been so successful within DuPont that the company has licensed Respect Inc. to sell "A Matter of Respect" to other companies. The company views "A Matter of Respect" as one component of its efforts to address the issue of diversity. DuPont also offers a wide range of training across levels, including a five-day multicultural workshop that deals with issues of race and gender in the workplace. A six-day course, "Efficacy for Minority Professionals," helps minority employees examine environmental and psychological obstacles to professional development. DuPont also has several corporate-wide minority employee networks. There are Asian, Hispanic, and black women's networks, as well as bisexual, gay/lesbian and allies at DuPont (BGLAD), and numerous other corporate employee networks.

Mentoring

Mentor relationships have always existed in the workplace. In a business context, mentors are generally seen as higher-level employees who can be depended upon to share personal insights and to provide guidance and support that can enhance performance and career development. A mentor may serve as a coach, instructing the protégé on what is needed to accomplish career objectives. A mentor may also act as a teacher, helping the protégé learn various organizational and professional skills and providing the protégé with information on how to "decode" the corporate culture. At times, the mentor may perform the role of protector, intervening or providing guidance to help the protégé manage difficult situations. Research has found that having a mentor can significantly affect an individual's career development and advancement. For example, in a 1986 study by Korn/Ferry International, an executive search firm, corporate leaders rated mentoring second only to education as a significant factor in their success. Two recent Catalyst studies, *On the Line: Women's Career Advancement* and *Women in Engineering: An Untapped Resource,* confirm that the coaching and advice women receive from influential colleagues are critical to their career advancement.

Unfortunately, research has also found that women face both interpersonal and organizational barriers to developing effective mentoring relationships. According to a 1990 U.S.

Department of Education study, the "screening mechanisms" used by mentors to select protégés result in women
having more difficulty attracting mentors than do men. One
researcher identified several obstacles for women in
obtaining a male mentor. These barriers include lack of
access to information networks, tokenism, stereotypes,
socialization practices, norms regarding cross-gender relationships and women's reliance on ineffective power bases
(Noe, 1988).

*Source: Catalyst, "Working with Business to Effect Change for
Women," report based on a study undertaken by Catalyst for the
Glass Ceiling Commission of the U.S. Department of Labor (1993),
Joyce Miller, Executive Director.

THREE: PERSONALIZE EDUCATION

Agreeing on terms, though, will mean little unless you are able to
educate your workforce. Education is the single most important
element in reducing sexual harassment in the workplace. And for the
education to do its job, it is crucial that management be committed to
the educational effort.

Approach employees in a manner that motivates them to want to
learn about something that is important to them and their own workplace. I suggest that education on this topic be built into a larger educational effort and be included in training efforts that blend the
company's philosophy, mission statement, and business goals into the
program. Understanding what this behavior is, how to respond to it,
and what the company's expectations are of each employee makes the
employees responsible for their own behavior and environment. The
company and the employees can begin to share the responsibility and,
in turn, accountability.

FOUR: ESTABLISH SOUND INTERNAL PROGRAMS

After the 1998 Supreme Court decisions, there is no question that companies must have a harassment policy in writing. But that is not enough. The policy should be understood by every employee, and it should be distributed often and be available everywhere the company does business. Policies are not just for the corporate or administrative offices of a company. One of the Supreme Court decisions involved a lifeguard on a beach; another involved a man on an oil rig out in the Gulf of Mexico. Sexual harassment policies cover people who work, and people work in all kinds of environments. A company's policy should protect everyone.

Make Sure Your Complaint Procedure Works. Most employees who choose not to report sexual harassment don't come forward because they don't believe their company has grievance procedures in place that will actually help them resolve their problem. Employees have charged that those appointed to hear complaints are not trained to investigate or evaluate those complaints. Others have felt that their company cannot conduct a fair and unbiased investigation. Many fear retaliation from both their company and the alleged harasser.

Be certain that those appointed to receive complaints know exactly what they are doing. Make sure they are trained for their role. Offer employees enough options for reporting sexual misconduct so that they do not have to fear immediate or long-term retaliation from anyone.

If employees know that their company has a strong grievance/complaint procedure in place and they believe in it, it will work as an effective means to greatly reducing sexual harassment in the workplace. I know of companies that have never had to face claims of sexual harassment that have reached the EEOC or the courts because their own internal processes have helped them resolve their own disputes.

AND THE POINT IS . . .

The President of the United States, although he survived, was impeached. The impeachment process came about, not because he had an affair with an intern, but because he was sued for sexual harassment and allegedly lied about his sexual behavior under oath. Yet what is interesting to me is the people's debate that continues to surround Clinton's recent predicament. Some say it's OK to lie about sexual behavior. Sex lives are a personal matter. He is a good president, so let us put aside his sexual appetite and poor judgment. Some ask us not to personally attack him. He did what any other guy would do in his situation. In fact, today's poll said that many Americans do not care whether or not a political leader has committed adultery.

National morality seems to be saying that personal lives and professional lives can be evaluated and kept separately. The problem that I have, particularly in my line of work, is that *this is precisely the point* when it comes to sexual harassment. Sexual harassment occurs because someone has *not separated* sexual or personal desires from their role and responsibilities within their workplace. Personal motives and private drives should not pass through the company's moral and ethical security detector and have their way in a workplace that belongs to people who have a right to work in an environment free of harassment and discrimination.

Notes and Sources

Introduction

Patrick McGeehan, "Judge Approves Class-Action Settlement for Sex Harassment at Smith Barney," *The Wall Street Journal*, July 27, 1998.

Chapter 1

"Sexual Harassment by Supervisors Is a Persistent Problem," *The Washington Post*, June 27, 1998, p. A10.

"The Perils of Flirtation," *The Economist*, February 14, 1998, pp. 25–26.

Hans Bader, "Free Speech Trumps Title VII Suits," *The National Law Journal*, November 24, 1997, p. A19.

Marianne Lavelle, "Sexual Harassment, the New Rules," *U.S. News & World Report*, July 6, 1998, pp. 30–31.

Jeffrey Rosen, "In Defense of Gender-Blindness," *The New Republic*, June 29, 1998, pp. 25–35.

Chapter 2

Richard Dooling, "Hey, Forget Justice, Let's All Just Sue!" *The National Law Journal*, July 20, 1998, p. A21.

Catherine A. MacKinnon, *Sexual Harassment of Working Women* (Yale University Press, New Haven, CT, 1979).

"Men, Women, Work and Law," *The Economist*, July 4, 1998, pp. 21–22.

Vicki Schultz, "Sex Is the Least of It, Let's Focus Harassment Law on Work, Not Sex," *The Nation*, May 25, 1998.

Deborah L. Jacobs, "When Boss' Office Affair Hurts You," Working Life, *Daily News*, July 2, 1995.

Art Buchwald, "The Harass Poll," *The Washington Post*, November 17, 1983, p. C1.

Harris v. Forklift Systems, Inc., 113 S. Ct., 1382, 122 L.Ed.2d 758 (1993).

Burlington Industries, Inc. v. Ellerth, S.Ct. 97-569 (1998).

"Firing for 'Seinfeld' Discussion Spurs Suit," Associated Press, June 26, 1997, p. 5B.

Ben Rand, "Too Many Cases, Too Few Caseworkers," *Gannett Suburban Newspapers,* December 21, 1996, p. 1.

From the Desk of Herbert Barchoff, "Sexual Harassment, in Uncertain Terms," *The New York Times,* January 26, 1997.

Tammy Joyner, "Office Romances Pose Indelicate Problems," *The Atlanta Journal-Constitution,* February 1, 1998, p. Q 9.

Chapter 3

Carolyn G. Heilbrun, "Writing a Woman's Life," (Ballantine Books, New York, 1988, pp. 44–46.

Celia Morris, *Bearing Witness: Sexual Harassment and Beyond—Everywoman's Story* (Little, Brown and Company, Boston, 1994).

"Study Raps Ways Sitcoms Portray Sex Harassment," *Boston Globe,* December 26, 1994, p. 39.

"On Television: Sexual Harassment Is Routine, Study Says," *Atlantic Constitution,* December 26, 1994, p. C9.

Dr. Elissa Perry, author's interview, August 1998.

Dr. Marion Gindes, author's interview, September 1998.

Chapter 4

Dr. Sandor Blum, author's interview, August 1998.

Susan L. Webb, *Step Forward: Sexual Harassment in the Workplace—What You Need to Know!* (MasterMedia, New York, 1991).

Betsy Morris, "Addicted to Sex," *Fortune* Magazine, May 10, 1999, pp. 67–76.

Kathleen Neville, *Sexual Harassment: Beyond the Law Leader's Guide* (corVision, Chicago, 1998).

Chapter 5

Kathleen Neville, *Corporate Attractions: An Inside Account of Sexual Harassment with the New Rules for Men and Women on the Job* (Acropolis Books, Washington, D.C., 1990).

Charles Kelly, "A Harsh Lesson on Harassment, NAU Staff Torn over 'Joke' Photo," *The Arizona Republic,* March 19, 1995, pp. A1, A18.

Libby Lewis, "Suit Blames Son's Suicide on AT&T," *Greensboro News & Observer,* July 24, 1994, pp. A1, A14.

Christopher Byron, "The Joke That Killed," *Esquire,* January 1995, pp. 83–90.

Del Jones, "Seinfeld Case Fallout, Award Creates Catch-22 for Companies," *USA Today,* July 17, 1997.

Lindsey Novak, "Loose Talk at Work, When Does an 'Inappropriate Comment' Become Sexual Harassment?" *Chicago Tribune,* September 20, 1998.

John Flesher, "Consequences of Web Publishing Can Backfire in Work Environment," Associated Press, January 16, 1998.

"Bias in the Workplace," *The Atlanta Journal-Constitution,* December 9, 1996, pp. E1, E12.

Chapter 7

Tony Jackson, "Grace Hit by Sexual Harassment Allegations," *Financial Times,* New York, March 31, 1995, p. 1.

Paul Tharp, "Axed Chief Threatens Suit over Sex Charge," *New York Post,* Business, March 31, 1995.

Angela G. King, "Women Criticize Grace for CEO's Severance Pay," *USA Today,* March 31, 1995.

Robert Moskowitz, "Sexual Harassment Suits Surge in Number—Charges against W. R. Grace Executive Sound Warning Bell," *Investor's Business Daily,* March 31, 1995, pp. 1–2.

"Grace, Ex-CEO Bolduc Spar over Harassment Charges," *Investor's Business Daily,* March 31, 1995.

Richard Gibson and Thomas M. Burton, "W. R. Grace Says Bolduc Resigned Because of Sex-Harassment Claim," *The Wall Street Journal,* March 31, 1995.

Judith H. Dobrzynski and Diana B. Henriques, "Grace Thrown into Turmoil over Sexual Harassment Allegations," *The New York Times,* Business, March 31, 1995, p. D3.

Elisabeth Rosenthal, "Hospital Chief Who Quit Denies Sexual Harassing of Employees," *The New York Times,* pp. A1, B4.

Diana B. Henriques, "Sexual Harassment and a Chief Executive," *The New York Times,* Business, March 30, 1995, pp. D1, D7.

Joann S. Lublin, "Attempts to Banish Harassment Reach into Executive Suite," *The Wall Street Journal,* March 31, 1995.

Thomas Burton, James P. Miller, and Richard Gibson, "Grace Chairman Resigns with 8 Others, Alleges a 'Scheme' to Force Him Out," *The Wall Street Journal,* April 7, 1995, p. A3.

William B. Falk, "Them vs. the CEO, the Women of Del Labs," *Newsday*, September 19, 1995, pp. A6–A7, A42–43.

Mark Marmont, "Abuse of Power—The Astonishing Tale of Sexual Harassment at Astra USA," *Business Week*, May 13, 1996, pp. 86–98.

Miriam Horn, "Sex & the CEO," *U.S. News & World Report*, July 6, 1998, pp. 32–40.

"Day of Reckoning at Astra," *Business Week*, July 7, 1996.

Chapter 9

"Mitsubishi Turmoil Continues in U.S. as Human Resources Manager Quits," *The Wall Street Journal*, November 4, 1997, p. 1.

"Mitsubishi Lawsuit Can Be Tried as Pattern, Practice Class Action," *The Wall Street Journal*, January 22, 1998.

Rochelle Sharpe, "Mitsubishi Unit Deceived Press, Ex-Official Says," *The Wall Street Journal*, January 12, 1998, p. A22.

"Mitsubishi Response to Sex Charges Creates More Problems Than It Solves," *Inside PR*, vol. 2, no. 28, May 6, 1996, pp. 1, 3.

"NOW Targets Smith Barney as First 'Merchant of Shame,' Calls All Employers to Take Women-Friendly Workplace Pledge," NOW web page, March 12, 1997.

"Sexual Harassment in the Fortune 500," *Working Woman*, December 1988; also "Sexual Harassment: The Inside Story," *Working Woman*, June 1992.

"Bottom Line Says It Pays to Care—Workers' Personal Lives Have Effect on Productivity, According to Study," *Gannett Newspapers*, February 19, 1997, p. 1E.

Ellen J. Wagner, *Sexual Harassment in the Workplace: How to Prevent, Investigate, and Resolve Problems in Your Organization* (Amacom, American Management Association, Creative Solutions, Inc., New York, 1992).

"Sexual Harassment Costs Go beyond the Courtroom," *Kansas City Business Journal*, April 18, 1997.

Sexual Harassment in Healthcare (Aspen Publishers, Inc., New York, 1997).

Margaret Stockdale, ed., *Sexual Harassment in the Workplace: Perspectives, Frontiers, and Response Strategies*, vol. 54 in *Women and Work* (Thousand Oaks, CA, Sage Publications, June 1998).

"How Does the Staying Power of a Firm's Reputation Affect Its Future Stock Market Performance?" Foundation for the School of Business at Indiana University, Bloomington, IN, 1998.

Barbara Gutek, *Women and Work 3: An Annual Review* (Thousand Oaks, CA, Sage Publications, 1988).

Barbara Gutek, "Understanding Sexual Harassment at Work," *Notre Dame Journal of Law & Ethics,* 1992.

"Study Shows Ethical Biz Is More Profitable," (DePaul University Study Reveals Financial Success of Companies with Ethical Business Practices,) *Accounting Today* (Faulkner & Gray, Inc., Chicago, 1997), p. 14.

Leslie Scism, "CNA Aides Quit As One Is Accused of Sex Harassment," *The Wall Street Journal,* March 5, 1997.

Joseph B. Treaster, "2 CNA Executives Quit in Sex Harassment Case," *The New York Times,* March 6, 1997.

Patrick McGeehan, "Judge Approves Class-Action Settlement for Sex Harassment at Smith Barney," *The Wall Street Journal,* July 27, 1998.

Peter Annin and John McCormick, "More Than a Tune-Up," *Newsweek,* November 24, 1997, pp. 50–51.

Ellen Goodman, "Harassment Is Not Only about Sex," *Boston Globe,* February 26, 1998.

Kristin Downey and Frank Swoboda, "Mitsubishi, EEOC Settle Lawsuit," *The Washington Post,* June 11, 1998, p. C1.

"Mitsubishi Steers in Wrong Direction with Lawsuit, Case Study," *PR News,* November 3, 1997, p. 5.

"Suitcases," *Newsweek,* September 29, 1997, p. 6.

Linda Greenhouse, "Sex Harassment Seems to Puzzle Supreme Court," *The New York Times,* April 23, 1998, pp. A1, A20.

Patrick McGeehan, "Two Analysts Leave Salomon in Smut Case," *The Wall Street Journal,* March 31, 1998, pp. C1, C25.

Peter Truell, "2 Executives Dismissed by Salomon over Pornography," *The New York Times,* March 31, 1998.

Chapter 10

Kathleen Neville, "On Firm Ground," *American Lawyer,* December 1997, pp. 36–37.

Joseph B. Treaster, "2 Executives in Harassment Case at CNA," *The New York Times,* Business, March 5, 1997, pp. 1, 22.

"Sexual Harassment Still Hush-Hush," *The Washington Post,* reprinted in *New York Newsday,* April 16, 1995.

Chapter 11

James Ang, "On Financial Ethics," *Financial Management,* September 22, 1993, p. 32.

Thomas A. Stewart with Ann Harrington and Maura Griffin Solovar, "America's Most Admired Companies: Why Leadership Matters," *Fortune*, March 2, 1998, pp. 70ff.

"Managing a Growing Risk: Employment Practices Liability," Guy Carpenter & Co. Inc., National Underwriter Company, November 1997.

John Naisbitt, *Global Paradox: The Bigger the World Economy, the More Powerful Its Smallest Players* (Morrow, New York, 1994).

Chapter 12

Philip Weiss, "No Sex, Please. This Is a Workplace," *The New York Times Magazine*, May 3, 1998, pp. 44–47.

William J. Bennett, *The Death of Outrage: Bill Clinton and the Assault on American Ideals* (The Free Press, New York, 1998).

Appendix

Supreme Court Decision Summaries

Civil Rights Act of 1991

Further Sources

Title VII of the Civil Rights Act of 1964

U.S. Equal Employment Opportunity Commission:
An Overview

Facts about Sexual Harassment

Filing a Charge

Facts about Federal Sector Equal Employment
Opportunity Complaint Processing Regulations

Example of One Company's
Sexual Harassment Policy

SUPREME COURT DECISION SUMMARIES
MERITOR SAVINGS BANK FSP V. VINSON (1986)

Michelle Vinson was hired as a teller-trainee. She was promoted to the position of assistant branch manager before she was fired by the bank for excessive use of sick leave. Vinson later sued the bank and her boss, Sidney Taylor, alleging hostile-environment sexual harassment. She claimed in her suit that her supervisor, Taylor, had forced her to have sex with him almost fifty times during her four years of employment. She claimed that he raped her, fondled her in front of other workers, and would even follow her into the bathroom. According to Court documents, the company did have a policy and complaint procedure, but she did not tap into any grievance channels because of her fear of retaliation by Taylor. The bank and the named offender defended themselves by saying that the relationship was consensual and voluntary, and that Vinson had never given them any kind of notice of unwanted sexual harassment. The Court ruled in favor of Vinson's claim of a hostile environment, and the case became the first Supreme Court ruling on sexual harassment.

A hostile or abusive work environment created to discriminate based on sex can be a violation of Title VII of the Civil Rights Act of 1964. To be cause for legal action the harassment must be severe enough to alter the conditions of the victim's employment (remarks that are offensive but not pervasive usually won't qualify). A sexual harassment claim does not have to involve negative economic effects on the victim. A crucial point in such cases is whether or not the harasser's sexual advances were unwelcome rather than whether or not the victim submitted voluntarily to the advances. Employers are not protected from liability merely because their organization has grievance procedures and antidiscrimination policies. And employers may be held liable for sexual harassment by their supervisory employees, even in cases in which the employers were not aware of the behavior, since employer liability for what supervisors do is automatic.

ONCALE, JOSEPH V. SUNDOWNER OFFSHORE, ET AL. (1998)

In this case, the U.S. Supreme Court ruled that same-sex harassment and male harassment claims can be brought under Title VII of the Civil Rights Act of 1964. The law protects men as well as women even if the harassment is by someone of the same sex, just as racial discrimination is available to all races even if the discrimination is by someone of the same race. However, the Court stated in very strong terms that Title VII is directed at discrimination because of sex, not merely conduct tinged with offensive sexual connotations. The statute does not reach innocuous differences in the ways men and women routinely interact with members of the opposite sex (or preferences now). And the objective severity of harassment should be judged from the perspective of a reasonable person in the plaintiff's position taking into consideration all the circumstances including the social context of the behavior, the surrounding circumstances, and the nature of the relationships involved. Workplace discrimination that is actionable must create a hostile environment in the terms or conditions of employment through intimidation, ridicule, or insult that would be considered a sufficiently severe or pervasive harassment to a reasonably objective person, and it must be sexual in content. The High Court noted, "We have always regarded those requirements as crucial, and as sufficient to ensure that courts and juries do not mistake ordinary socializing in the workplace—such as male-on-male horseplay or inter-sexual flirtation for discriminatory conditions of employment." The concerns that harassment rulings will transform Title VII into a general civility code for the

American workplace are "adequately met by careful attention to the requirements of the statute. Title VII does not prohibit all verbal or physical harassment in the workplace: it is directed only at discrimination . . . because of . . . sex." There must be "disadvantageous" terms or conditions to which other members of the other sex are not exposed." In this case, the male plaintiff worked on an offshore oil rig and claimed he was touched, grabbed, verbally abused, and repeatedly threatened with rape by other members of the all-male crew. His complaints to the company were essentially ignored, and superiors acknowledged prior similar conduct. Note that this ruling does not decide the case itself. It only allows the case to go forward in court.

U.S. SUPREME COURT ENDS 1998 TERM WITH THREE SEXUAL HARASSMENT RULINGS (FROM THE WASHINGTONPOST.COM)

BURLINGTON INDUSTRIES V. ELLERTH

Court ruled that employers are liable for the unwelcome and threatening sexual advances of a supervisor, even if the threats are not carried out and the harassed employee suffers no adverse, tangible effects.

FARRAGHER V. BOCA RATON, FLA

Court ruled that an employer is potentially liable for harassment by a supervisor.

GEBSER V. LAGO VISTA INDEPENDENT SCHOOL DISTRICT

School districts are not responsible if teachers sexually harass or abuse students and school administrators do not know about it.

The U.S. Supreme Court decided three cases involving sexual harassment issues during the final full week of June 1998. These cases followed one prior ruling this year in this still developing area of the law, allowing claims for same sex harassment. These three cases clarify some of the circumstances in which claims can be brought but largely leave the definition of sexual harassment to prior decisions. The Court held that under Title VII certain employers can be held vicariously responsible to pay damages caused to employees for even unknown and non-negligent instances by the employer when a supervisor intentionally acts to create a sexually hostile work place by sexual conduct that is so severe and pervasive that it substantially interferes with the employees' conditions of employment. However, the cases encourage employers to develop and make known to all employees the policies and procedures aimed at reducing and resolving sexual harassment problems by providing a potential affirmative defense to completely cut off the exposure for vicarious liability for unknown acts of supervisors. The defense is provided to the employer when reasonable anti-harassment and corrective steps are established to be available by the evidence and the claimant has failed to take reasonable steps to utilize and/or comply with those available methods or company procedures. By establishing the affirmative defense for employers the cases specifically increase the requirement that claimants take reasonable steps to avoid, report and respond to circumstances where they perceive potential wrongful conduct is occurring, before it rises to the severity of creating an actual hostile work place and legally damaging them. The affirmative defense created by the cases is not available in quid pro quo cases which require that a definite adverse or negative tangible job detriment has in fact taken place or occurred under the authority of a harassing supervisor and carried out by the employer (denial of promotion or pay raise, etc.). In the case of only being threatened by unfulfilled job detriments made by a supervisor to demand or coerce sex or acceptance of sexual harassment conduct, the Court explained that the requirements for "hostile environment" claims must be alleged and proven after overcoming the new affirmative defense before a recovery of damages can be made. Thus if an employee unreasonably complies with threats demanding sex or allowing alleged improper sexual conduct instead of taking reasonable actions to stop or avoid the problem, which actions the employee knows or reasonably should know exist and are available including (but not limited to) complying with known company rules or likely capabilities to correct the situation and other related procedures, the claim will be defeated in court. The focus of the law is to improve the workplace, not encourage people to participate in allowing (or even helping to foster) wrongful conduct and then file lawsuits to obtain their pay from litigation. The Court decided in the case of a school district under Title IX a private claim for monetary damages cannot be brought by a student for sexual harassment of a teacher or other lower level district employees unless the conduct is actually known by certain district officials who intentionally fail to take corrective measures.

CIVIL RIGHTS ACT OF 1991

The key provisions of the Civil Rights Act of 1991 signed November 21, 1991, were that jury trials be available for complainants and that compensatory damages (based upon intentional discrimination and unlawful employment practice) and punitive damages (based upon the size of the employer) may be awarded in successful suits.

- This act allows up to $300,000 in compensatory and punitive damages in addition to reinstatement, back pay, and injunctive relief.
- It also allows for attorney fees for the plaintiff.

FURTHER SOURCES
ORGANIZATIONS

American Association of University Women
1111 16th Street, NW
Washington, D.C. 20036

American Bar Association
Women in the Profession
750 N. Lake Shore Drive
Chicago, Illinois 60611

Coalition of Labor Union Women
1126 16th Street, NW
Washington, D.C. 20036

corVision Media
1359 Barclay Boulevard
Buffalo Grove, Illinois 60089
800-537-3100
Sexual harassment videos/leadership guides

Hill and Knowlton
466 Lexington Avenue
New York, New York 10017
Virtual crisis on sexual harassment

National Women and the Law Association
1810 Sixth Street
Berkeley, California 94710
Publishes the *National Women's Legal Directory,* a listing by state of lawyers, law
    firms, and women's rights organizations that specialize in issues of concern to
    women

National Employment Lawyers Association
535 Pacific Avenue
San Francisco, California 94133

9 to 5
National Association of Working Women
614 Superior Avenue NW

Cleveland, Ohio 44114-2649
800-522-0925
Maintains a toll-free job problem hotline that provides information and advice on work-related concerns for over 60,000 working women a year

Xcape, Inc.
37 Holsman Road
Staten Island, New York 10301-4426
Interactive/on-line training for companies

PUBLICATIONS

Clark, Charles S., "Sexual Harassment: Men and Women in Workplace Power Struggles," *CQ Researcher,* vol. 1, no. 13, August 9, 1991.

"Preventing Sexual Harassment" Perspective, *Catalyst,* February 1992.

Responses of Fair Employment Practices Agencies to Sexual Harassment Complaints: A Report and Recommendations (Working Women's United Institute, New York, 1978).

Sandler, Bernice R., "Sexual Harassment: A New Issue for Institutions," *Initiatives,* vol. 52, no. 4, Winter 1990.

Sexual Harassment Manual for Managers and Supervisors (Commerce Clearing House, Chicago, 1991).

Sexual Harassment: Research and Resources (The National Council for Research on Women, New York, 1991).

U.S. Merit Systems Protection Board, *Sexual Harassment of Federal Workers: Is it a Problem?* (U.S. Government Printing Office, Washington, D.C., 1987).

TITLE VII OF THE CIVIL RIGHTS ACT OF 1964

EDITOR'S NOTE: The following is the text of Title VII of the Civil Rights Act of 1964 (Pub. L. 88-352) (Title VII), as amended, as it appears in volume 42 of the United States Code, beginning at section 2000e. Title VII prohibits employment discrimination based on race, color, religion, sex, and national origin. The Civil Rights Act of 1991 (Pub. L. 102-166) (CRA) amends several sections of Title VII. These amendments appear in boldface type. In addition, section 102 of the CRA (which is printed elsewhere in this publication) amends the Revised Statutes by adding a new section following section 1977 (42 U.S.C. 1981), to provide for the recovery of compensatory and punitive damages in cases of intentional violations of Title VII, the Americans with Disabilities Act of 1990, and section 501 of the Rehabilitation Act of 1973. Cross-references to Title VII as enacted appear in italics following each section heading. Editor's notes also appear in italics.

AN ACT

To enforce the constitutional right to vote, to confer jurisdiction upon the district courts of the United States to provide injunctive relief against discrimination in public accommodations, to authorize the Attorney General to institute suits to protect constitutional rights in public facilities and public education, to extend the Commission on Civil Rights, to prevent discrimination in federally assisted programs, to establish a Commission on Equal Employment Opportunity, and for other purposes.

Be it enacted by the Senate and House of Representatives of the United States of America in Congress assembled, That this Act may be cited as the "Civil Rights Act of 1964."

DEFINITIONS

SEC. 2000e. [Section 701]
For the purposes of this subchapter—
(a) The term "person" includes one or more individuals, governments, governmental agencies, political subdivisions, labor unions, partner-

ships, associations, corporations, legal representatives, mutual companies, joint-stock companies, trusts, unincorporated organizations, trustees, trustees in cases under title 11 [bankruptcy], or receivers.

(b) The term "employer" means a person engaged in an industry affecting commerce who has fifteen or more employees for each working day in each of twenty or more calendar weeks in the current or preceding calendar year, and any agent of such a person, but such term does not include (1) the United States, a corporation wholly owned by the Government of the United States, an Indian tribe, or any department or agency of the District of Columbia subject by statute to procedures of the competitive service (as defined in section 2102 of title 5 [of the United States Code]), or (2) a bona fide private membership club (other than a labor organization) which is exempt from taxation under section 501(c) of title 26 [the Internal Revenue Code of 1954], except that during the first year after March 24, 1972 [the date of enactment of the Equal Employment Opportunity Act of 1972], persons having fewer than twenty-five employees (and their agents) shall not be considered employers.

(c) The term "employment agency" means any person regularly undertaking with or without compensation to procure employees for an employer or to procure for employees opportunities to work for an employer and includes an agent of such a person.

(d) The term "labor organization" means a labor organization engaged in an industry affecting commerce, and any agent of such an organization, and includes any organization of any kind, any agency, or employee representation committee, group, association, or plan so engaged in which employees participate and which exists for the purpose, in whole or in part, of dealing with employers concerning grievances, labor disputes, wages, rates of pay, hours, or other terms or conditions of employment, and any conference, general committee, joint or system board, or joint council so engaged which is subordinate to a national or international labor organization.

(e) A labor organization shall be deemed to be engaged in an industry affecting commerce if (1) it maintains or operates a hiring hall or hiring office which procures employees for an employer or procures for employees opportunities to work for an employer, or (2) the number of its members (or, where it is a labor organization composed of other labor organizations or their representatives, if the aggregate number of the members of such other labor organization) is (A) twenty-five or more during the first year after March 24, 1972 [the date of enactment of the Equal Employment Opportunity Act of 1972], or (B) fifteen or more thereafter, and such labor organization—

(1) is the certified representative of employees under the provisions of the National Labor Relations Act, as amended [29 U.S.C. 151 et seq.], or the Railway Labor Act, as amended [45 U.S.C. 151 et seq.];

(2) although not certified, is a national or international labor organization or a local labor organization recognized or acting as the representative of employees of an employer or employers engaged in an industry affecting commerce; or

(3) has chartered a local labor organization or subsidiary body which is representing or actively seeking to represent employees of employers within the meaning of paragraph (1) or (2); or

(4) has been chartered by a labor organization representing or actively seeking to represent employees within the meaning of paragraph (1) or (2) as the local or subordinate body through which such employees may enjoy membership or become affiliated with such labor organization; or

(5) is a conference, general committee, joint or system board, or joint council subordinate to a national or international labor organization, which includes a labor organization engaged in an industry affecting commerce within the meaning of any of the preceding paragraphs of this subsection.

(f) The term "employee" means an individual employed by an employer, except that the term "employee" shall not include any person elected to public office in any State or political subdivision of any State by the qualified voters thereof, or any person chosen by such officer to be on such officer's personal staff, or an appointee on the policy making level or an immediate adviser with respect to the exercise of the constitutional or legal powers of the office. The exemption set forth in the preceding sentence shall not include employees subject to the civil service laws of a State government, governmental agency or political subdivision. With respect to employment in a foreign country, such term includes an individual who is a citizen of the United States.

(g) The term "commerce" means trade, traffic, commerce, transportation, transmission, or communication among the several States; or between a State and any place outside thereof; or within the District of Columbia, or a possession of the United States; or between points in the same State but through a point outside thereof.

(h) The term "industry affecting commerce" means any activity, business, or industry in commerce or in which a labor dispute would hinder or obstruct commerce or the free flow of commerce and includes any activity or industry "affecting commerce" within the meaning of the Labor-Management Reporting and Disclosure Act of 1959 [29 U.S.C. 401 et seq.], and further includes any governmental industry, business, or activity.

(i) The term "State" includes a State of the United States, the District of Columbia, Puerto Rico, the Virgin Islands, American Samoa, Guam, Wake Island, the Canal Zone, and Outer Continental Shelf lands defined in the Outer Continental Shelf Lands Act [43 U.S.C. 1331 et seq.].

(j) The term "religion" includes all aspects of religious observance and practice, as well as belief, unless an employer demonstrates that he is unable to reasonably accommodate to an employee's or prospective employee's religious observance or practice without undue hardship on the conduct of the employer's business.

(k) The terms "because of sex" or "on the basis of sex" include, but are not limited to, because of or on the basis of pregnancy, childbirth, or related medical conditions; and women affected by pregnancy, childbirth, or related medical conditions shall be treated the same for all employment-related purposes, including receipt of benefits under fringe benefit programs, as other persons not so affected but similar in their ability or inability to work, and nothing in section 2000e-2(h) of this title [section 703(h)] shall be interpreted to permit otherwise. This subsection shall not require an employer to pay for health insurance benefits for abortion, except where the life of the mother would be endangered if the fetus were carried to term, or except where medical complications have arisen from an abortion: Provided, That nothing herein shall preclude an employer from providing abortion benefits or otherwise affect bargaining agreements in regard to abortion.

(l) The term "complaining party" means the Commission, the Attorney General, or a person who may bring an action or proceeding under this subchapter.

(m) The term "demonstrates" means meets the burdens of production and persuasion.

(n) The term "respondent" means an employer, employment agency, labor organization, joint labor-management committee controlling apprenticeship or other training or retraining program, including an on-the-job training program, or Federal entity subject to section 2000e-16 of this title.

EXEMPTION

SEC. 2000e-1. [Section 702]

(a) This subchapter shall not apply to an employer with respect to the employment of aliens outside any State, or to a religious corporation, association, educational institution, or society with respect to the employment of individuals of a particular religion to perform work connected with the carrying on by such corporation, association, educational institution, or society of its activities.

(b) It shall not be unlawful under section 2000e-2 or 2000e-3 of this title [section 703 or 704] for an employer (or a corporation controlled by an employer), labor organization, employment agency, or joint labor-management committee controlling apprenticeship or other training or retraining (including on-the-job training programs) to take any action otherwise prohibited by such section, with respect to an employee in a workplace in a foreign country if compliance with such section would cause such employer (or such corporation), such organization, such agency, or such committee to violate the law of the foreign country in which such workplace is located.

(c) (1) If an employer controls a corporation whose place of incorporation is a foreign country, any practice prohibited by section 2000e-2 or 2000e-3 of this title [section 703 or 704] engaged in by such corporation shall be presumed to be engaged in by such employer.

(2) Sections 2000e-2 and 2000e-3 of this title [sections 703 and 704] shall not apply with respect to the foreign operations of an employer that is a foreign person not controlled by an American employer.

(3) For purposes of this subsection, the determination of whether an employer controls a corporation shall be based on—

(A) the interrelation of operations;

(B) the common management;

(C) the centralized control of labor relations; and

(D) the common ownership or financial control, of the employer and the corporation.

UNLAWFUL EMPLOYMENT PRACTICES

SEC. 2000e-2 [Section 703]

(a) It shall be an unlawful employment practice for an employer—

(1) to fail or refuse to hire or to discharge any individual, or otherwise to discriminate against any individual with respect to his compensation, terms, conditions, or privileges of employment, because of such individual's race, color, religion, sex, or national origin; or

(2) to limit, segregate, or classify his employees or applicants for employment in any way which would deprive or tend to deprive any individual of employment opportunities or otherwise adversely affect his status as an employee, because of such individual's race, color, religion, sex, or national origin.

(b) It shall be an unlawful employment practice for an employment agency to fail or refuse to refer for employment, or otherwise to discriminate against, any individual because of his race, color, religion, sex, or national origin, or to classify or refer for employment any individual on the basis of his race, color, religion, sex, or national origin.

(c) It shall be an unlawful employment practice for a labor organization—

(1) to exclude or to expel from its membership, or otherwise to discriminate against, any individual because of his race, color, religion, sex, or national origin;

(2) to limit, segregate, or classify its membership or applicants for membership, or to classify or fail or refuse to refer for employment any individual, in any way which would deprive or tend to deprive any individual of employment opportunities, or would limit such employment opportunities or otherwise adversely affect his status as an employee or as an applicant for employment, because of such individual's race, color, religion, sex, or national origin; or

(3) to cause or attempt to cause an employer to discriminate against an individual in violation of this section.

(d) It shall be an unlawful employment practice for any employer, labor organization, or joint labor-management committee controlling apprenticeship or other training or retraining, including on-the-job training programs to discriminate against any individual because of his race, color, religion, sex, or national origin in admission to, or employment in, any program established to provide apprenticeship or other training.

(e) Notwithstanding any other provision of this subchapter, (1) it shall not be an unlawful employment practice for an employer to hire and employ employees, for an employment agency to classify, or refer for employment any individual, for a labor organization to classify its membership or to classify or refer for employment any individual, or for an employer, labor organization, or joint labor-management committee controlling apprenticeship or other training or retraining programs to admit or employ any individual in any such program, on the basis of his religion, sex, or national origin in those certain instances where religion, sex, or national origin is a bona fide occupational qualification reasonably necessary to the normal operation of that particular business or enterprise, and (2) it shall not be an unlawful employment practice for a school, college, university, or other educational institution or institution of learning to hire and employ employees of a particular religion if such school, college, university, or other educational institution or institution of learning is, in whole or in substantial part, owned, supported, controlled, or managed by a particular religion or by a particular religious corporation, association, or society, or if the curriculum of such school, college, university, or other educational institution or institution of learning is directed toward the propagation of a particular religion.

(f) As used in this subchapter, the phrase "unlawful employment practice" shall not be deemed to include any action or measure taken by an employer, labor organization, joint labor-management committee, or employment agency with respect to an individual who is a member of the Communist Party of the United States or of any other organization required to register as a Communist-action or Communist-front organization by final order of the Subversive Activities Control Board pursuant to the Subversive Activities Control Act of 1950 [50 U.S.C. 781 et seq.].

(g) Notwithstanding any other provision of this subchapter, it shall not be an unlawful employment practice for an employer to fail or refuse to hire and employ any individual for any position, for an employer to discharge any individual from any position, or for an employment agency to fail or refuse to refer any individual for employment in any position, or for a labor organization to fail or refuse to refer any individual for employment in any position, if—

(1) the occupancy of such position, or access to the premises in or upon which any part of the duties of such position is performed or is to be performed, is subject to any requirement imposed in the interest of the national security of the United States under any security program in effect pursuant to or administered under any statute of the United States or any Executive order of the President; and

(2) such individual has not fulfilled or has ceased to fulfill that requirement.

(h) Notwithstanding any other provision of this subchapter, it shall not be an unlawful employment practice for an employer to apply different standards of compensation, or different terms, conditions, or privileges of employment pursuant to a bona fide seniority or merit system, or a system which measures earnings by quantity or quality of production or to employees who work in different locations, provided that such differences are not the result of an intention to discriminate because of race, color, religion, sex, or national origin, nor shall it be an unlawful employment practice for an employer to give and to act upon the results of any professionally developed ability test provided that such test, its administration or action upon the results is not designed, intended or used to discriminate because of race, color, religion, sex or national origin. It shall not be an unlawful employment practice under this subchapter for any employer to differentiate upon the basis of sex in determining the amount of the wages or compensation paid or to be paid to employees of such employer if such differentiation is authorized by the provisions of section 206(d) of title 29 [section 6(d) of the Fair Labor Standards Act of 1938, as amended].

(i) Nothing contained in this subchapter shall apply to any business or enterprise on or near an Indian reservation with respect to any publicly announced employment practice of such business or enterprise under which a preferential treatment is given to any individual because he is an Indian living on or near a reservation.

(j) Nothing contained in this subchapter shall be interpreted to require any employer, employment agency, labor organization, or joint labor-management committee subject to this subchapter to grant preferential treatment to any individual or to any group because of the race, color, religion, sex, or national origin of such individual or group on account of an imbalance which may exist with respect to the total number or percentage of persons of any race, color, religion, sex, or national origin employed by any employer, referred or classified for employment by any employment agency or labor organization, admitted to membership or classified by any labor organization, or admitted to, or employed in, any apprenticeship or other training program, in comparison with the total number or percentage of persons of such race, color, religion, sex, or national origin in any community, State, section, or other area, or in the available work force in any community, State, section, or other area.

(k) (1) (A) An unlawful employment practice based on disparate impact is established under this title only if—

> (i) a complaining party demonstrates that a respondent uses a particular employment practice that causes a disparate impact on the basis of race, color, religion, sex, or national origin and the respondent fails to demonstrate that the challenged practice is job related for the position in question and consistent with business necessity; or

> (ii) the complaining party makes the demonstration

described in subparagraph (C) with respect to an alternative employment practice and the respondent refuses to adopt such alternative employment practice.

(B) (i) With respect to demonstrating that a particular employment practice causes a disparate impact as described in subparagraph (A)(i), the complaining party shall demonstrate that each particular challenged employment practice causes a disparate impact, except that if the complaining party can demonstrate to the court that the elements of a respondent's decisionmaking process are not capable of separation for analysis, the decisionmaking process may be analyzed as one employment practice.

(ii) If the respondent demonstrates that a specific employment practice does not cause the disparate impact, the respondent shall not be required to demonstrate that such practice is required by business necessity.

(C) The demonstration referred to by subparagraph (A)(ii) shall be in accordance with the law as it existed on June 4, 1989, with respect to the concept of "alternative employment practice."

(2) A demonstration that an employment practice is required by business necessity may not be used as a defense against a claim of intentional discrimination under this title.

(3) Notwithstanding any other provision of this title, a rule barring the employment of an individual who currently and knowingly uses or possesses a controlled substance, as defined in schedules I and II of section 102(6) of the Controlled Substances Act (21 U.S.C. 802(6)), other than the use or possession of a drug taken under the supervision of a licensed health care professional, or any other use or possession authorized by the Controlled Substances Act [21 U.S.C. 801 et seq.] or any other provision of Federal law, shall be considered an unlawful employment practice under this title only if such rule is adopted or applied with an intent to discriminate because of race, color, religion, sex, or national origin.

(l) It shall be an unlawful employment practice for a respondent, in connection with the selection or referral of applicants or candidates for employment or promotion, to adjust the scores of, use different cutoff scores for, or otherwise alter the results of, employment related tests on the basis of race, color, religion, sex, or national origin.

(m) Except as otherwise provided in this title, an unlawful employment practice is established when the complaining party demonstrates that race, color, religion, sex, or national origin was a motivating factor for any employment practice, even though other factors also motivated the practice.

(n) (1) (A) Notwithstanding any other provision of law, and except as provided in paragraph (2), an employment practice that implements and is within the scope of a litigated or consent judgment or order that resolves a claim of employment discrimination under the Constitution or Federal civil rights laws may not be challenged under the circumstances described in subparagraph (B).

> (B) A practice described in subparagraph (A) may not be challenged in a claim under the Constitution or Federal civil rights laws—

>> (i) by a person who, prior to the entry of the judgment or order described in subparagraph (A), had—

>>> (I) actual notice of the proposed judgment or order sufficient to apprise such person that such judgment or order might adversely affect the interests and legal rights of such person and that an opportunity was available to present objections to such judgment or order by a future date certain; and

>>> (II) a reasonable opportunity to present objections to such judgment or order; or

>> (ii) by a person whose interests were adequately represented by another person who had previously challenged the judg-

ment or order on the same legal grounds and with a similar factual situation, unless there has been an intervening change in law or fact.

(2) Nothing in this subsection shall be construed to—

(A) alter the standards for intervention under rule 24 of the Federal Rules of Civil Procedure or apply to the rights of parties who have successfully intervened pursuant to such rule in the proceeding in which the parties intervened;

(B) apply to the rights of parties to the action in which a litigated or consent judgment or order was entered, or of members of a class represented or sought to be represented in such action, or of members of a group on whose behalf relief was sought in such action by the Federal Government;

(C) prevent challenges to a litigated or consent judgment or order on the ground that such judgment or order was obtained through collusion or fraud, or is transparently invalid or was entered by a court lacking subject matter jurisdiction; or

(D) authorize or permit the denial to any person of the due process of law required by the Constitution.

(3) Any action not precluded under this subsection that challenges an employment consent judgment or order described in paragraph (1) shall be brought in the court, and if possible before the judge, that entered such judgment or order. Nothing in this subsection shall preclude a transfer of such action pursuant to section 1404 of title 28, United States Code.

OTHER UNLAWFUL EMPLOYMENT PRACTICES

SEC. 2000e-3. [Section 704]

(a) It shall be an unlawful employment practice for an employer to discriminate against any of his employees or applicants for employment, for an employment agency, or joint labor-management committee controlling apprenticeship or other training or retraining, including on-the-job training programs, to discriminate against any individual, or for a labor organization to discriminate against any member thereof or applicant for membership, because he has opposed any practice made an unlawful employment practice by this subchapter, or because he has made a charge, testified, assisted, or participated in any manner in an investigation, proceeding, or hearing under this subchapter.

(b) It shall be an unlawful employment practice for an employer, labor organization, employment agency, or joint labor-management committee controlling apprenticeship or other training or retraining, including on-the-job training programs, to print or publish or cause to be printed or published any notice or advertisement relating to employment by such an employer or membership in or any classification or referral for employment by such a labor organization, or relating to any classification or referral for employment by such an employment agency, or relating to admission to, or employment in, any program established to provide apprenticeship or other training by such a joint labor-management committee, indicating any preference, limitation, specification, or discrimination, based on race, color, religion, sex, or national origin, except that such a notice or advertisement may indicate a preference, limitation, specification, or discrimination based on religion, sex, or national origin when religion, sex, or national origin is a bona fide occupational qualification for employment.

EQUAL EMPLOYMENT OPPORTUNITY COMMISSION

SEC. 2000e-4. [Section 705]

(a) There is hereby created a Commission to be known as the Equal Employment Opportunity Commission, which shall be composed of five members, not more than three of whom shall be members of the same political party. Members of the Commission shall be appointed by the President by and with the advice and consent of the Senate for a term of five years. Any individual chosen to fill a vacancy shall be appointed only for the unexpired term of the member whom he shall succeed, and all members of the Commission shall continue to serve until their successors are appointed and qualified, except that no such member of the Commission shall continue to serve (1) for more than sixty days when the Congress is in session unless a nomination to fill such vacancy shall have been submitted to the Senate, or (2) after the adjournment sine die of the session of the Senate in which such nomination was submitted. The President shall designate one member to serve as Chairman of the Commission, and one member to serve as Vice Chairman. The Chairman shall be responsible on behalf of the Commission for the administrative operations of the Commission, and, except as provided in subsection (b) of this section, shall appoint, in accordance with the provisions of title 5 [United States Code] governing appointments in the competitive service, such officers, agents, attorneys, administrative law judges [hearing examiners], and employees as he deems necessary to assist it in the performance of its functions and to fix their compensation in accordance with the provisions of chapter 51 and subchapter III of chapter 53 of title 5 [United States Code], relating to classification and General Schedule pay rates: Provided, That assignment, removal, and compensation of administrative law judges [hearing examiners] shall be in accordance with sections 3105, 3344, 5372, and 7521 of title 5 [United States Code].

(b) (1) There shall be a General Counsel of the Commission appointed by the President, by and with the advice and consent of the Senate, for a term of four years. The General Counsel shall have responsibility for the conduct of litigation as provided in sections 2000e-5 and 2000e-6 of this title [sections 706 and 707]. The General Counsel shall have such other duties as the Commission may prescribe or as may be provided by law and shall concur with the Chairman of the Commission on the appointment and supervision of regional attorneys. The General

Counsel of the Commission on the effective date of this Act shall continue in such position and perform the functions specified in this subsection until a successor is appointed and qualified.

(2) Attorneys appointed under this section may, at the direction of the Commission, appear for and represent the Commission in any case in court, provided that the Attorney General shall conduct all litigation to which the Commission is a party in the Supreme Court pursuant to this subchapter.

(c) A vacancy in the Commission shall not impair the right of the remaining members to exercise all the powers of the Commission and three members thereof shall constitute a quorum.

(d) The Commission shall have an official seal which shall be judicially noticed.

(e) The Commission shall at the close of each fiscal year report to the Congress and to the President concerning the action it has taken [the names, salaries, and duties of all individuals in its employ] and the moneys it has disbursed. It shall make such further reports on the cause of and means of eliminating discrimination and such recommendations for further legislation as may appear desirable.

(f) The principal office of the Commission shall be in or near the District of Columbia, but it may meet or exercise any or all its powers at any other place. The Commission may establish such regional or State offices as it deems necessary to accomplish the purpose of this subchapter.

(g) The Commission shall have power—

(1) to cooperate with and, with their consent, utilize regional, State, local, and other agencies, both public and private, and individuals;

(2) to pay to witnesses whose depositions are taken or who are summoned before the Commission or any of its agents the same witness and mileage fees as are paid to witnesses in the courts of the United States;

(3) to furnish to persons subject to this subchapter such technical assistance as they may request to further their compliance with this subchapter or an order issued thereunder;

(4) upon the request of (i) any employer, whose employees or some of them, or (ii) any labor organization, whose members or some of them, refuse or threaten to refuse to cooperate in effectuating the provisions of this subchapter, to assist in such effectuation by conciliation or such other remedial action as is provided by this subchapter;

(5) to make such technical studies as are appropriate to effectuate the purposes and policies of this subchapter and to make the results of such studies available to the public;

(6) to intervene in a civil action brought under section 2000e-5 of this title [section 706] by an aggrieved party against a respondent other than a government, governmental agency or political subdivision.

(h) (1) The Commission shall, in any of its educational or promotional activities, cooperate with other departments and agencies in the performance of such educational and promotional activities.

(2) In exercising its powers under this title, the Commission shall carry out educational and outreach activities (including dissemination of information in languages other than English) targeted to—

(A) individuals who historically have been victims of employment discrimination and have not been equitably served by the Commission; and

(B) individuals on whose behalf the Commission has authority to enforce any other law prohibiting employment discrimination, concerning rights and obligations under this title or such law, as the case may be.

(i) All officers, agents, attorneys, and employees of the Commission shall be subject to the provisions of section

7324 of title 5 [section 9 of the Act of August 2, 1939, as amended (the Hatch Act)], notwithstanding any exemption contained in such section.

(j) (1) The Commission shall establish a Technical Assistance Training Institute, through which the Commission shall provide technical assistance and training regarding the laws and regulations enforced by the Commission.

(2) An employer or other entity covered under this title shall not be excused from compliance with the requirements of this title because of any failure to receive technical assistance under this subsection.

(3) There are authorized to be appropriated to carry out this subsection such sums as may be necessary for fiscal year 1992.

ENFORCEMENT PROVISIONS

SEC. 2000e-5. [Section 706]

(a) The Commission is empowered, as hereinafter provided, to prevent any person from engaging in any unlawful employment practice as set forth in section 2000e-2 or 2000e-3 of this title [section 703 or 704].

(b) Whenever a charge is filed by or on behalf of a person claiming to be aggrieved, or by a member of the Commission, alleging that an employer, employment agency, labor organization, or joint labor-management committee controlling apprenticeship or other training or retraining, including on-the-job training programs, has engaged in an unlawful employment practice, the Commission shall serve a notice of the charge (including the date, place and circumstances of the alleged unlawful employment practice) on such employer, employment agency, labor organization, or joint labor-management committee (hereinafter referred to as the "respondent") within ten days, and shall make an investigation thereof. Charges shall be in writing under oath or affirmation and shall contain such information and be in such form as the Commission requires. Charges shall not be made public by the

Commission. If the Commission determines after such investigation that there is not reasonable cause to believe that the charge is true, it shall dismiss the charge and promptly notify the person claiming to be aggrieved and the respondent of its action. In determining whether reasonable cause exists, the Commission shall accord substantial weight to final findings and orders made by State or local authorities in proceedings commenced under State or local law pursuant to the requirements of subsections (c) and (d) of this section. If the Commission determines after such investigation that there is reasonable cause to believe that the charge is true, the Commission shall endeavor to eliminate any such alleged unlawful employment practice by informal methods of conference, conciliation, and persuasion. Nothing said or done during and as a part of such informal endeavors may be made public by the Commission, its officers or employees, or used as evidence in a subsequent proceeding without the written consent of the persons concerned. Any person who makes public information in violation of this subsection shall be fined not more than $1,000 or imprisoned for not more than one year, or both. The Commission shall make its determination on reasonable cause as promptly as possible and, so far as practicable, not later than one hundred and twenty days from the filing of the charge or, where applicable under subsection (c) or (d) of this section, from the date upon which the Commission is authorized to take action with respect to the charge.

(c) In the case of an alleged unlawful employment practice occurring in a State, or political subdivision of a State, which has a State or local law prohibiting the unlawful employment practice alleged and establishing or authorizing a State or local authority to grant or seek relief from such practice or to institute criminal proceedings with respect thereto upon receiving notice thereof, no charge may be filed under subsection (a) of this section by the person aggrieved before the expiration of sixty days after proceedings have been commenced under the State or local law, unless such proceedings have been earlier terminated, provided that such sixty-day period shall be extended to one hundred and twenty days during the first year after the effective date of such State or local law. If any requirement for the commencement of such proceedings is imposed by a State or local authority other than a requirement of the filing of a written and signed statement of the facts upon which the proceeding is based, the proceeding shall be deemed to have been commenced for the purposes of this subsection at the time such statement is sent by registered mail to the appropriate State or local authority.

(d) In the case of any charge filed by a member of the Commission alleging an unlawful employment practice occurring in a State or political subdivision of a State which has a State or local law prohibiting the practice alleged and establishing or authorizing a State or local authority to grant or seek relief from such practice or to institute criminal proceedings with respect thereto upon receiving notice thereof, the Commission shall, before taking any action with respect to such charge, notify the appropriate State or local officials and, upon request, afford them a reasonable time, but not less than sixty days (provided that such sixty-day period shall be extended to one hundred and twenty days during the first year after the effective day of such State or local law), unless a shorter period is requested, to act under such State or local law to remedy the practice alleged.

(e) (1) A charge under this section shall be filed within one hundred and eighty days after the alleged unlawful employment practice occurred and notice of the charge (including the date, place and circumstances of the alleged unlawful employment practice) shall be served upon the person against whom such charge is made within ten days thereafter, except that in a case of an unlawful employment practice with respect to which the person aggrieved has initially instituted proceedings with a State or local agency with authority to grant or seek relief from such practice or to institute criminal proceedings with respect thereto upon receiving notice thereof, such charge shall be filed by or on behalf of the person aggrieved within three hundred days after the alleged unlawful employment practice occurred, or within thirty days after receiving notice that the State or local agency has terminated the proceedings under the State or local law, whichever is earlier, and a copy of such charge shall be filed by the Commission with the State or local agency.

(2) For purposes of this section, an unlawful employment practice occurs, with respect to a seniority system that has been adopted for an intentionally discriminatory purpose in violation of this title (whether or not that discriminatory purpose is apparent on the face of the seniority provision), when the seniority system is adopted, when an individual becomes subject to the seniority system, or when a person aggrieved is injured by the application of the seniority system or provision of the system.

(f) (1) If within thirty days after a charge is filed with the Commission or within thirty days after expiration of any period of reference under subsection (c) or (d) of this section, the Commission has been unable to secure from the respondent a conciliation agreement acceptable to the Commission, the Commission may bring a civil action against any respondent not a government, governmental agency, or political subdivision named in the charge. In the case of a respondent which is a government, governmental agency, or political subdivision, if the Commission has been unable to secure from the respondent a conciliation agreement acceptable to the Commission, the Commission shall take no further action and shall refer the case to the Attorney General who may bring a civil action against such respondent in the appropriate United States district court. The person or persons aggrieved shall have the right to intervene in a civil action brought by the Commission or the Attorney General in a case involving a government, governmental agency, or political subdivision. If a charge filed with the Commission pursuant to subsection (b) of this section, is dismissed by the Commission, or if within one hundred and eighty days from the filing of such charge or the expiration of any period of reference under subsection (c) or (d) of this section, whichever is later, the Commission has not filed a civil action under this section or the Attorney General has not filed a civil action in a case involving a government, governmental agency, or political subdivision, or the Commission has not entered into a conciliation agreement to which the person aggrieved is a party, the Commission, or the Attorney General in a case involving a government, governmental agency, or political subdivision, shall so notify the person aggrieved and within ninety days after the giving of such notice a civil action may be brought against the respondent named in the charge (A) by the person claiming to be aggrieved or (B) if such charge was filed by a member of the Commission, by any person whom the charge alleges was aggrieved by the alleged unlawful employment practice. Upon application by the complainant and in such circumstances as the court may deem just, the court may appoint an attorney for such complainant and may authorize the commencement of the action without the payment of fees, costs, or security. Upon timely application, the court may, in its discretion, permit the Commission, or the Attorney General in a case involving a government, governmental agency, or political subdivision, to intervene in such civil action upon certification that the case is of general public importance. Upon request, the court may, in its discretion, stay further proceedings for not more than sixty days pending the termination of State or local proceedings described in subsection (c) or (d) of this section or further efforts of the Commission to obtain voluntary compliance.

(2) Whenever a charge is filed with the Commission and the Commission concludes on the basis of a preliminary investigation that prompt judicial action is necessary to carry out the purposes of this Act, the Commission, or the Attorney General in a case involving a government, governmental agency, or political subdivision, may bring an action for appropriate temporary or preliminary relief pending final disposition of such charge. Any temporary restraining order or other order granting preliminary or temporary relief shall be issued in accordance with rule 65 of the Federal Rules of Civil

Procedure. It shall be the duty of a court having jurisdiction over proceedings under this section to assign cases for hearing at the earliest practicable date and to cause such cases to be in every way expedited.

(3) Each United States district court and each United States court of a place subject to the jurisdiction of the United States shall have jurisdiction of actions brought under this subchapter. Such an action may be brought in any judicial district in the State in which the unlawful employment practice is alleged to have been committed, in the judicial district in which the employment records relevant to such practice are maintained and administered, or in the judicial district in which the aggrieved person would have worked but for the alleged unlawful employment practice, but if the respondent is not found within any such district, such an action may be brought within the judicial district in which the respondent has his principal office. For purposes of sections 1404 and 1406 of title 28 [of the United States Code], the judicial district in which the respondent has his principal office shall in all cases be considered a district in which the action might have been brought.

(4) It shall be the duty of the chief judge of the district (or in his absence, the acting chief judge) in which the case is pending immediately to designate a judge in such district to hear and determine the case. In the event that no judge in the district is available to hear and determine the case, the chief judge of the district, or the acting chief judge, as the case may be, shall certify this fact to the chief judge of the circuit (or in his absence, the acting chief judge) who shall then designate a district or circuit judge of the circuit to hear and determine the case.

(5) It shall be the duty of the judge designated pursuant to this subsection to assign the case for hearing at the earliest practicable date and to cause the case to be in every way expedited. If such judge has not scheduled the case for trial within one hundred and twenty

days after issue has been joined, that judge may appoint a master pursuant to rule 53 of the Federal Rules of Civil Procedure.

(g) (1) If the court finds that the respondent has intentionally engaged in or is intentionally engaging in an unlawful employment practice charged in the complaint, the court may enjoin the respondent from engaging in such unlawful employment practice, and order such affirmative action as may be appropriate, which may include, but is not limited to, reinstatement or hiring of employees, with or without back pay (payable by the employer, employment agency, or labor organization, as the case may be, responsible for the unlawful employment practice), or any other equitable relief as the court deems appropriate. Back pay liability shall not accrue from a date more than two years prior to the filing of a charge with the Commission. Interim earnings or amounts earnable with reasonable diligence by the person or persons discriminated against shall operate to reduce the back pay otherwise allowable.

(2) (A) No order of the court shall require the admission or reinstatement of an individual as a member of a union, or the hiring, reinstatement, or promotion of an individual as an employee, or the payment to him of any back pay, if such individual was refused admission, suspended, or expelled, or was refused employment or advancement or was suspended or discharged for any reason other than discrimination on account of race, color, religion, sex, or national origin or in violation of section 2000e-3(a) of this title [section 704(a)].

(B) On a claim in which an individual proves a violation under section 2000e-2(m) of this title [section 703(m)] and a respondent demonstrates that the respondent would have taken the same action in the absence of the impermissible motivating factor, the court—

(i) may grant declaratory relief, injunctive relief (except as provided in clause (ii)), and attorney's fees and costs demonstrated to be directly attributable only to the pursuit of a claim under section 2000e-2(m) of this title [section 703(m)]; and

(ii) shall not award damages or issue an order requiring any admission, reinstatement, hiring, promotion, or payment, described in subparagraph (A).

(h) The provisions of chapter 6 of title 29 [the Act entitled "An Act to amend the Judicial Code and to define and limit the jurisdiction of courts sitting in equity, and for other purposes," approved March 23, 1932 (29 U.S.C. 105-115)] shall not apply with respect to civil actions brought under this section.

(i) In any case in which an employer, employment agency, or labor organization fails to comply with an order of a court issued in a civil action brought under this section, the Commission may commence proceedings to compel compliance with such order.

(j) Any civil action brought under this section and any proceedings brought under subsection (i) of this section shall be subject to appeal as provided in sections 1291 and 1292, title 28 [United States Code].

U.S. EQUAL EMPLOYMENT OPPORTUNITY COMMISSION: AN OVERVIEW

MISSION

The mission of the EEOC, as set forth in its strategic plan, is to promote equal opportunity in employment through administrative and judicial enforcement of the federal civil rights laws and through education and technical assistance.

STATUTORY AUTHORITY

The U.S. Equal Employment Opportunity Commission (EEOC) was established by Title VII of the Civil Rights Act of 1964 and began operating on July 2, 1965. The EEOC enforces the principal federal statutes prohibiting employment discrimination, including:

- Title VII of the Civil Rights Act of 1964, as amended, which prohibits employment discrimination on the basis of race, color, religion, sex, or national origin;

- the Age Discrimination in Employment Act of 1967, as amended (ADEA), which prohibits employment discrimination against individuals 40 years of age and older;

- the Equal Pay Act of 1963 (EPA), which prohibits discrimination on the basis of gender in compensation for substantially similar work under similar conditions;

- the Title I of the Americans with Disabilities Act of 1990 (ADA), which prohibits employment discrimination on the basis of disability in both the public and private sector, excluding the federal government;

- the Civil Rights Act of 1991, which includes provisions for monetary damages in cases of intentional discrimination and clarifies provisions regarding disparate impact actions; and,

- Section 501 of the Rehabilitation Act of 1973, as amended, which prohibits employment discrimination against federal employees with disabilities.

EEOC ENFORCEMENT ACTIVITIES

Overview   The EEOC carries out its work at headquarters and in 50 field offices throughout the United States. Individuals who believe they have been discriminated against in employment begin our processes by filing administrative charges. Individual Commissioners may also initiate charges that the law has been violated. Through the investigation of charges, if the EEOC determines there is "reasonable cause" to believe that discrimination has occurred, it must then seek to conciliate the charge to reach a voluntary resolution between the charging party and the respondent. If conciliation is not successful, the EEOC may bring suit in federal court. Whenever the EEOC concludes its processing of a case, or earlier upon the request of a charging party, it issues a "notice of right to sue" which enables the charging party to bring an individual action in court.

The Commission also issues regulatory and other forms of guidance interpreting the laws it enforces, is responsible for the federal sector employment discrimination program, provides funding and support to state and local fair employment practices agencies (FEPAs), and conducts broad-based outreach and technical assistance programs.

Administrative Enforcement   EEOC's strategically designed administrative enforcement program effectively manages between 75,000 and 80,000 charges that are filed annually. Under the Commission's charge processing system:

- Charges are prioritized into one of three categories for purposes of investigation and resource allocation. "Category A" charges are priority charges to which offices devote principal investigative and settlement efforts. "Category B" charges are those where there appears to be some merit but more investigation is needed before a decision is made on handling. "Category C" charges include non-jurisdictional, self-defeating, or unsupported charges which are immediately closed.

- Settlements are encouraged at all stages of the process.

- The EEOC has launched a mediation-based alternative dispute resolution (ADR) program. The mediation program is guided by principles of informed and voluntary participation at all stages, confidential deliberation by all parties, and neutral mediators.

As a direct result of these initiatives:

- By the end of fiscal year 1998, EEOC's pending inventory was

52,011 charges, a decline of 53 percent from an all-time high of 111,345 in the third quarter of fiscal year 1995.

- In fiscal year 1998, the Commission was continuing to resolve charges at a faster pace than they were being filed, further reducing the inventory.

- In fiscal year 1998, the Agency obtained $169.2 million in monetary benefits for charging parties (excluding litigation awards) through settlement and conciliation. Commissioner charges accounted for $2.1 million of this total.

- The EEOC has made substantial progress in the implementation of its mediation program. From the inception of the program in fiscal year 1996 through the end of fiscal year 1998, EEOC resolved over 2,400 charges through mediation and obtained benefits of approximately $27.8 million for charging parties.

National Enforcement Plan   In February 1996, the Commission approved its National Enforcement Plan (NEP), which sets out a three-pronged framework for the Commission's enforcement strategy: prevention of discrimination through education and outreach; the voluntary resolution of disputes where possible; and where voluntary resolution fails, strong and fair enforcement. The NEP also identifies priority areas for EEOC investigation and litigation, delegates certain litigation decisions to the General Counsel, and directs the EEOC field offices to develop Local Enforcement Plans (LEPs) which tailor the mandates of the NEP to the particular needs and issues of their communities.

Litigation   The EEOC's litigation program has achieved significant results in the past few years under the NEP. In fiscal year 1996, the EEOC obtained over $50 million in monetary benefits for discrimination victims. In fiscal year 1997, the amount rose to $111 million in benefits, and represents the largest annual recovery in EEOC history. In fiscal year 1998, the EEOC's litigation program recovered nearly $90 million for victims of discrimination. The EEOC also files amicus curiae or "friend of the court" briefs in trial and Appellate Courts in support of the Commission's position, usually in cases involving novel issues. In fiscal year 1998, the Commission filed 70 such briefs. Among the EEOC's recent litigation achievements are:

- an age bias settlement with Lockheed Martin (formerly Martin Marietta) for $13 million in back pay and 450 jobs for older workers who were dismissed;

- settlement of race/national origin/sex bias claims against a major supermarket chain in Texas for $2.5 million in back pay and over 5,000 entry-level and 34 management trainee job offers to qualified African American, Hispanic, and female applicants previously denied positions;

- a $34 million settlement in a sexual harassment case with Mitsubishi Motor Manufacturing of America, and a settlement of almost $10 million in a sexual harassment case against Astra USA Inc., a pharmaceutical company in Massachusetts—the EEOC's two largest sexual harassment settlements to date. These cases are notable for Mitsubishi's adoption of extensive changes to its sexual harassment prevention policy and complaint procedure, and Astra's issuance of formal apologies to the women involved; and

- under the ADA, a $5.5 million jury verdict for an employee who was discharged from his job because he has epilepsy, and a $3.5 million jury verdict for a paraplegic job applicant denied a job at Wal-Mart after being told the store had "no openings for a person in a wheelchair." Although both amounts will be reduced based on the statutory cap on damages, the juries' verdicts represent the two largest ADA awards in EEOC history, and send a powerful message to those who would discriminate on the basis of disability.

State and Local Program   The EEOC contracts with approximately 90 FEPAs to process more than 48,000 discrimination charges annually. These charges raise claims under state and local laws prohibiting employment discrimination as well as the federal laws enforced by the EEOC.

Federal Sector Program   The EEOC is responsible for enforcing the anti-discrimination laws in the federal sector. The EEOC conducts thousands of hearings every year for federal employees who have filed discrimination complaints. In addition, when a federal agency issues a final decision on a complaint of discrimination, the complainant can appeal that decision to the EEOC. In fiscal year 1998, the EEOC received 12,218 requests for administrative hearings and resolved 7,494 appeals.

The Commission also ensures that the federal departments and agencies maintain programs of equal employment opportunity required under Title VII and the Rehabilitation Act. Moreover, under Executive Order 12067, the Commission provides leadership and coordination to all federal departments' and agencies' programs enforcing statutes, executive orders, regulations, and policies which require equal employment opportunity or which have equal employment opportunity implications.

Outreach Activities   In fiscal year 1997, the EEOC launched a home page on the Internet to provide the public with greater access to an array of agency information materials and resources. The new home page can be found on the World Wide Web at http://www.eeoc.gov/. Information included on the home page consists of Annual Reports, addresses and phone numbers of field offices, press releases, fact sheets, and periodicals. Early in fiscal year 1998, the EEOC also added a small business information fact sheet to its web site, highlighting select issues of particular interest to small businesses.

During fiscal year 1997, the EEOC almost doubled the number in annual Technical Assistance Program Seminars (TAPS), offering 65 seminars educating over 8,000 individuals in the private sector and state and local governments about EEOC enforced laws. In fiscal year 1998, EEOC conducted 58 TAPS, reaching 7,100 participants. Agency staff made over 2,100 public presentations, reaching over 87,000 people during fiscal year 1998, and responded to thousands of requests for technical assistance. The EEOC responded to over 100,000 requests from the public, distributing over 450,000 publications, with ADA-related information many in alternative formats making up nearly one fourth of the responses.

BUDGET AND STAFFING

- The EEOC's fiscal year 1998 budget appropriation was $242,000,000, including $27.5 million for payments to the FEPAs. For fiscal year 1999, Congress approved the President's request for $279,000,000, including $29 million for the FEPAs.

- Due to limited budgets throughout the 1980's and into the 90's, the EEOC's complement of full time employees fell from a high of 3,390 in 1980, to 2,544 at the end of fiscal year 1998. The decline in resources came at the same time the agency's enforcement obligations substantially expanded due to new statutory responsibilities. Charges under the ADA, enacted in 1990, currently account for nearly one quarter of EEOC's case-load. In addition, charge filings increased following the enact-ment of the Civil Rights Act of 1991. The increase has been particularly dramatic with regard to sexual harassment charges. Overall, charge filings have jumped from 62,135 in fiscal year 1990 to around 80,000 in both fiscal years 1997 and 1998.

- Approximately 90% of the agency's budget is allocated to fixed costs such as salaries, benefits, and rent. This is due to the highly personnel intensive nature of the EEOC's work in investigating, resolving, and litigating charges. However, it also means that only 10% of the agency's budget is available for such critically important functions as litigation support, technology, and staff training.

Office of Communications and Legislative Affairs

November 1998

FACTS ABOUT SEXUAL HARASSMENT

Sexual harassment is a form of sex discrimination that violates *Title VII of the Civil Rights Act of 1964.*

Unwelcome sexual advances, requests for sexual favors, and other verbal or physical conduct of a sexual nature constitutes sexual harassment when submission to or rejection of this conduct explicitly or implicitly affects an individual's employment, unreasonably interferes with an individual's work performance or creates an intimidating, hostile or offensive work environment.

Sexual harassment can occur in a variety of circumstances, including but not limited to the following:

- The victim as well as the harasser may be a woman or a man. The victim does not have to be of the opposite sex.
- The harasser can be the victim's supervisor, an agent of the employer, a supervisor in another area, a co-worker, or a non-employee.
- The victim does not have to be the person harassed but could be anyone affected by the offensive conduct.
- Unlawful sexual harassment may occur without economic injury to or discharge of the victim.
- The harasser's conduct must be unwelcome.

It is helpful for the victim to directly inform the harasser that the conduct is unwelcome and must stop. The victim should use any employer complaint mechanism or grievance system available.

When investigating allegations of sexual harassment, EEOC looks at the whole record: the circumstances, such as the nature of the sexual advances, and the context in which the alleged incidents occurred. A determination on the allegations is made from the facts on a case-by-case basis.

Prevention is the best tool to eliminate sexual harassment in the workplace. Employers are encouraged to take steps necessary to prevent sexual harassment from occurring. They should clearly communicate to employees that sexual harassment will not be tolerated. They can do so by establishing an effective complaint or grievance process and taking immediate and appropriate action when an employee complains.

THE U.S. EQUAL EMPLOYMENT OPPORTUNITY COMMISSION

FILING A CHARGE

Federal Employees: Please see our fact sheet on *Federal Sector Equal Employment Opportunity Complaint Processing.*

If you believe you have been discriminated against by an employer, labor union or employment agency when applying for a job or while on the job because of your **race, color, sex, religion, national origin, age,** or **disability,** or believe that you have been discriminated against because of opposing a prohibited practice or participating in an equal employment opportunity matter, you may file a charge of discrimination with the U.S. Equal Employment Opportunity Commission (EEOC).

Charges may be filed in person, by mail or by telephone by *contacting the nearest EEOC office.* If there is not an EEOC office in the immediate area, call toll free 800-669-4000 or 800-669-6820 (TDD) for more information. To avoid delay, call or write beforehand if you need special assistance, such as an interpreter, to file a charge.

There are strict time frames in which charges of employment discrimination must be filed. To preserve the ability of EEOC to act on your behalf and to protect your right to file a private lawsuit, should you ultimately need to, adhere to the following guidelines when filing a charge.

Title VII of the Civil Rights Act (Title VII)— Charges must be filed with EEOC within 180 days of the alleged discriminatory act. However, in states or localities where there is an antidiscrimination law and an agency authorized to grant or seek relief, a charge must be presented to that state or local agency. Furthermore, in such jurisdictions, you may file charges with EEOC within 300 days of the discriminatory act, or 30 days after receiving notice that the state or local agency has terminated its processing of the charge, whichever is earlier. It is best to contact EEOC promptly when discrimination is suspected. When charges or complaints are filed beyond these time frames, you may not be able to obtain any remedy.

Americans with Disabilities Act (ADA)— The time requirements for filing a charge are the same as those for Title VII charges.

Age Discrimination in Employment Act (ADEA)— The time requirements for filing a charge are the same as those for Title VII and the ADA.

Equal Pay Act (EPA)— Individuals are not required to file an EPA charge with EEOC before filing a private lawsuit. However, charges may be filed with EEOC and some cases of wage discrimination also may be violations of Title VII. If an EPA charge is filed with EEOC, the procedure for filing is the same as for charges brought under Title VII. However, the time limits for filing in court are different under the EPA, thus, it is advisable to file a charge as soon as you become aware the EPA may have been violated.

For more detailed information, please *contact the EEOC office nearest to you.*

THE U.S. EQUAL EMPLOYMENT OPPORTUNITY COMMISSION

FACTS ABOUT FEDERAL SECTOR EQUAL EMPLOYMENT OPPORTUNITY COMPLAINT PROCESSING REGULATIONS (29 CFR PART 1614)

Part 1614 of the federal sector equal employment opportunity complaint processing regulations replaces part 1613, with the objective of promoting greater administrative fairness in the investigation and consideration of federal sector EEO complaints by creating a process that is quicker and more efficient.

STATUTES COVERED BY 1614 REGULATIONS

Title VII of the Civil Rights Act of 1964 makes it illegal to discriminate in employment based on race, color, religion, sex or national origin.

Section 501 of the Rehabilitation Act of 1973 makes it illegal to discriminate against federal employees and applicants for employment based on disability. Federal agencies are required to make reasonable accommodations to the known physical and mental limitations of qualified employees or applicants with disabilities. Section 501 also requires affirmative action for hiring, placement and promotion of qualified individuals with disabilities.

The Equal Pay Act   prohibits employers from discriminating on the basis of sex in the payment of wages where substantially equal work is performed under similar working conditions.

The Age Discrimination in Employment Act   protects people 40 years of age and older by prohibiting age discrimination in hiring, discharge, pay, promotions and other terms and conditions of employment.

RETALIATION/REPRISAL

A person who files a complaint or charge, participates in an investigation or charge, or opposes an employment practice made illegal by any of the above statutes is protected from retaliation.

FILING A COMPLAINT WITH A FEDERAL AGENCY

The first step for an employee or applicant who feels he or she has been discriminated against by a federal agency is to contact an equal employment opportunity counselor at the agency where the alleged discrimination took place within 45 days of the discriminatory action. Ordinarily, counseling must be completed within 30 days. The aggrieved individual may then file a complaint with that agency.

The agency must acknowledge or reject the complaint and if it does not dismiss it, the agency must, within 180 days, conduct a complete and fair investigation.

If the complaint is one that does not contain issues that are appealable to the Merit Systems Protection Board (MSPB), at the conclusion of the investigation, the complainant may request either a hearing by an Equal Employment Opportunity Commission (EEOC) administrative judge (AJ) or an immediate final decision by the employing agency.

The AJ must process the request for a hearing, issue findings of fact and conclusions of law, and order an appropriate remedy within 180 days.

After the final decision of the agency, the complainant may appeal to the Commission within 30 days or may file in U.S. District Court within 90 days. Either party may request reconsideration by the Commission. The complainant may seek judicial review.

FILING AN APPEAL WITH THE EEOC

If the agency dismisses all or part of a complaint, a dissatisfied complainant may file an expedited appeal, within 30 days of notice of the dismissal, with the EEOC. The EEOC may determine that the dismissal was improper, reverse the dismissal, and remand the matter back to the agency for completion of the investigation.

A complainant may also appeal a final agency decision to the EEOC within 30 days of notice of the decision. The EEOC will examine the record and issue decisions.

If the complaint is on a matter that is appealable to the Merit Systems Protection Board (e.g., a mixed case such as a termination of a career employee), the complainant may appeal the final agency decision to the MSPB within 20 days of receipt or go to U.S. District Court within 30 days. The complainant may petition the EEOC for review of the MSPB decision concerning the claim of discrimination.

REMEDIES

The EEOC's policy is to seek full and effective relief for each and every victim of discrimination. These remedies may include:

- posting a notice to all employees advising them of their rights under the laws EEOC enforces and their right to be free from retaliation;

- corrective or preventive actions taken to cure or correct the source of the identified discrimination;

- nondiscriminatory placement in the position the victim would have occupied if the discrimination had not occurred;

- compensatory damages;

- back pay (with interest where applicable), lost benefits;

- stopping the specific discriminatory practices involved; and

- recovery of reasonable attorney's fees and costs.

Information on all EEOC-enforced laws may be obtained by calling toll free on 800-669-EEOC. EEOC's toll free TDD number is 800-800-3302. This fact sheet is also available in alternate formats, upon request.

January 1994
EEOC-FS/E-7

EXAMPLE OF ONE COMPANY'S SEXUAL HARASSMENT POLICY

It is the goal of [employer] to promote a workplace that is free of sexual harassment. Sexual harassment of employees occurring in the workplace and other settings in which employees may find themselves in connection with their employment is unlawful and will not be tolerated by [employer]. Further, any retaliation against an individual who has complained about sexual harassment or retaliation against individuals for cooperating with an investigation of a sexual harassment complaint is similarly unlawful and will not be tolerated.

To achieve our goal of providing a workplace free of sexual harassment, the conduct that is described in this policy will not be tolerated and we have provided a procedure by which inappropriate conduct will be dealt with, if encountered by employees. Because [employer] takes allegations of sexual harassment seriously, we will respond promptly to complaints of sexual harassment and where it is determined that such inappropriate conduct has occurred, we will act promptly to eliminate the conduct and impose such corrective action as is necessary, including disciplinary action where appropriate.

Please note, while this policy sets forth our goals of promoting a workplace that is free of sexual harassment, the policy is not designed or intended to limit our authority to discipline or take remedial action for workplace conduct which we deem unacceptable, regardless of whether that conduct satisfies the definition of sexual harassment.

DEFINITION OF SEXUAL HARASSMENT:

The legal definition for sexual harassment is:

"unwelcome sexual advances or requests for sexual favors or any other verbal or physical contact of a sexual nature when submission to, or such conduct or advances or requests is made either explicitly or implicitly a term or condition of an individual's employment."

It is also sexual harassment when such advances, requests, or conduct have the purpose or effect of unreasonably interfering with an individual's work performance by creating an intimidating, hostile, humiliating or sexually offensive work environment.

Under these definitions, direct or implied requests by a supervisor for sexual favors in exchange for actual or promised job benefits such as favorable reviews, salary increases, promotions, increased benefits, or continued employment constitutes sexual harassment. The legal definition of sexual harassment is broad and other sexually oriented conduct, whether it is intended or not, that is unwelcome and has the effect of creating a work place environment that is hostile, offensive, intimidating, or humiliating to male or female workers may also constitute sexual harassment.

While it is not possible to list all those additional circumstances that may constitute sexual harassment, the following are some examples of conduct which, if unwelcome, may constitute depending upon the totality of the circumstances including the severity of the conduct and its pervasiveness:

- Unwelcome sexual advances—whether they involve physical touching or not;
- Sexual epithets, jokes, written or oral references to sexual conduct, gossip regarding one's sex life; comment on another individual's body, comment about an individual's sexual activity, deficiencies, or prowess;
- displaying sexually suggestive objects, pictures, or cartoons;
- Unwelcome leering, whistling, brushing against the body, sexual gestures, suggestive or insulting comments;
- Inquiries into one's sexual experiences; and
- Discussion of one's sexual activities.

All employees should take special note that, as stated above, retaliation against an individual who has complained about sexual harassment, and retaliation against individuals for cooperating with an investigation of a sexual harassment complaint is unlawful and will not be tolerated by [employer].

COMPLAINTS OF SEXUAL HARASSMENT

If any employee believes that he/she has been subjected to sexual harassment, the employee has the right to file a complaint with [employer]. This may be done orally or in writing.

If you would like to file a complaint, you may do so by contacting:

[insert contact names, addresses, and telephone numbers]

These persons are also available to discuss any concerns you may have and to provide information to you about our policy on sexual harassment and our complaint process.

SEXUAL HARASSMENT INVESTIGATION

When we receive the complaint, we will promptly investigate the complaint in a fair and expeditious manner. The investigation will be conducted in such a way as to maintain confidentiality to the extent practicable under the circumstances. Our investigation will include a private interview with the person filing the complaint and the witnesses. We will also interview the person alleged to have committed sexual harassment. When we have completed our investigation, we will, to the extent appropriate, inform the person filing the complaint and the person alleging to have committed the conduct of the results of that investigation.

DISCIPLINARY ACTION

If it is determined that inappropriate conduct has been committed by one of our employees, we will take such action as is appropriate under the circumstances. Such action may range from counseling to termination of employment, and may include such other forms of disciplinary action as we deem appropriate under the circumstances.

STATE AND FEDERAL DISCRIMINATION ENFORCEMENT AGENCIES

In addition to the above, if you believe you have been subjected to sexual harassment, you may file a formal complaint with either or both of the government agencies set forth below. Using our complaint process does not prohibit you from filing a complaint with these agencies.

The United States Equal Employment Opportunity Commission (EEOC)

State Human Rights Agency

Index